ENERGY POLICY

Energy Policy
An Economic Analysis

⟡⟡⟡⟡⟡⟡

Paul W. MacAvoy

W · W · NORTON & COMPANY
NEW YORK   LONDON

The text of this book is composed in Times Roman.
Composition and manufacturing by The Maple-Vail Book Manufacturing Group.

Library of Congress Cataloging in Publication Data
MacAvoy, Paul W.
    Energy policy.
    Bibliography: p.
    Includes index.
    1. Energy policy—Economic aspects—United States.
    2. United States—Economic policy—1981–
    I. Title.
HD9502.U52M34   1983   333.79'0973   82–24551

ISBN 0-393-01723-0

ISBN 0-393-95321-1 pbk.

W. W. Norton & Company, Inc.,
500 Fifth Avenue, New York, N.Y. 10110
W. W. Norton & Company, Ltd.,
37 Great Russell Street, London WC1B 3NU

2 3 4 5 6 7 8 9 0

Contents

List of Tables

◇◇◇◇◇

4. Service Quality and Regulation in Retail Electricity and Gas

5. Energy Policy for the 1980s

Preface

◇◇◇◇◇

Policy studies of the energy sector of the American economy abound. Many are quite good and some are excellent—particularly Hans Landsberg's *Energy: The Next Twenty Years* and S. H. Schurr's *Energy in America's Future: The Choices Before Us*.[1] These describe the conditions of energy markets at the end of the 1970s and propose new policy for the next five to fifty years to improve operations of these markets.

Then why one more book on energy policy? The answer is that additional evaluation of present policy is needed at this time because present policy is much more likely to become future policy than the proposals in the Landsberg and Schurr books. The performance of the rules and regulations created after the OPEC embargo of 1973–1974 should be evaluated because they will likely be in place and thus will determine the condition of the energy sector of the economy over much of the decade of the 1980s.

This study completes such an economic analysis of existing energy policy. While proposed new policies are dealt with in the concluding chapter, the general presumption is that most policy

1. Cf. Hans Landsberg, *Energy: The Next Twenty Years* (Cambridge, Mass.: Ballinger, 1979); and S. H. Schurr, *Energy in America's Future: The Choices Before Us* (Baltimore and London: Johns Hopkins University Press, published for Resources for the Future, 1979).

developments in the 1980s will spring from existing statutes and regulatory practices. Thus the continuing conduct of Congress, the ongoing rules issued by agencies in the Executive Office, and the current decisions of the courts are evaluated as *de facto* ''energy policy'' by means of the generally useful tools of economic theory and statistical analysis.

The major finding from the evaluation is that consistent and indeed almost uniform effects follow from the various regulatory policies developed for each of the different fuels. Congress and the White House have tended to adopt certain uniform regulatory practices in order to contain the effects of fuel scarcity on prices charged final consumers. These practices have not worked well, and in the face of short-term supply interruptions, have been highly counterproductive for the consuming economy. Yet they have not been terminated and such policies are still well established at the beginning of the 1980s. Thus the outlook for the energy sector is not encouraging.

The findings presented in this volume are based on research undertaken over a number of years. Earlier stages of the research results were reported in P. W. MacAvoy, *Crude Oil Prices: As Determined by OPEC and Market Fundamentals* (Cambridge, Mass.: Ballinger, 1982); P. W. MacAvoy and Andrew S. Carron, *The Decline of Service in the Regulated Industries* (Washington, D.C.: American Enterprise Institute, 1981); P. W. MacAvoy, *The Regulated Industries and the Economy* (New York: W. W. Norton, 1979); and P. W. MacAvoy, ''The Natural Gas Policy Act of 1978,'' *Natural Resources Journal* (December 1979). The most recent stages have been undertaken as a project of the Research Program in Government-Business Relations of the Yale School of Organization and Management. Substantial funding was provided by the Olin Foundation, the J.M. Foundation, the General Electric Foundation, and the Walker Foundation in support of this research program. Assistance in conducting the recent work was provided by the Olin Fellows in that program, particularly Scott Cantor, Eric Murphy, Jon Chambers, and Richard Brummell. James Dana assisted with the construction of the gas model in

Chapter 3. Denise McMillan provided valuable assistance throughout, especially in obtaining the new data and completing the most recent appraisals of petroleum product price regulations in Chapter 2 and of electricity regulations in Chapter 4.

Improvements of this work have been demanded by my critics. Paul Joskow of the Massachusetts Institute of Technology furnished an invaluable critique of the working-paper draft of this manuscript, and specifically called for reevaluation of effects of petroleum regulations along lines indicated in the footnotes on his views in Chapter 2. Andrew Carron of the Brookings Institution, Milton Russell of Resources for the Future, and Joseph Kalt of Harvard University provided considerable assistance in completing the economic analyses in Chapters 2, 3, and 4. They called for attaining higher standards in research, and I am grateful for their urging along these lines. Much is owed to all of these individuals and organizations for expanding the opportunities for me to produce a comprehensive review of the present energy policy condition.

Paul W. MacAvoy

ENERGY POLICY

1

<small>⬦⬦⬦⬦</small>

Energy Policy and Economics

THE PAST DECADE brought forth more new energy policy than any comparable period since World War II. This was the reaction to sharp energy sector shocks. Crude oil price increases after the OPEC crude oil embargo of 1974 had substantial adverse impacts on manufacturing and trade throughout the economy. Natural gas shortages that developed from domestic price controls had similar impacts at the same time. In response to this supply stringency in crude oil and natural gas markets, the federal government imposed numerous new regulations on those fuels. At the same time severe and sustained application of established rate-regulation principles to electricity and gas distribution transformed regulation in those industries.

But in the early 1980s, even after another round of supply shocks, there has been much less development of new policy. Rather than "don't just stand there, do something" the reverse has been the new practice. This is because there has been an improvement in the performance of the energy sector over that realized in the past decade without further policy development. Furthermore, it is widely believed that the problems created by the new policy of the 1970s exceeded those solved, so that if history is repeated less government intervention could very well reduce the energy problems of the 1980s.

Such critical beliefs are evaluated here with regard to (1)

soundness of policy objectives, (2) the success of the policy in achieving its stated objectives, and (3) the additional problems and costs created by the policy itself. A balanced analysis should consider all three elements, weighing the degrees of success and failure in each in determining effectiveness. But the motivation to initiate a policy and the selection of policy goals are chiefly political matters, produced by the interaction of various social and economic interests. These are taken here as given, and policy performance rather than formulation is evaluated, with the behavior of energy markets indicating the successes and failures. Economic measures of policy performance include effects on relative prices, the availability of supplies, the efficient allocation of energy resources, and income distribution. In the pages to follow, the efficacy of the energy policies of the 1970s is evaluated with regard to intended and unintended consequences for these economic variables.

This chapter provides an overview of the major policy initiatives. Subsequent chapters deal in more detail with the policies applied to the petroleum, natural gas production, and retail gas and electricity industries. The last chapter draws on these case studies to determine the prospects for the energy sector and for better policy in the 1980s.

Energy Markets in the 1970s

It was clear early in the decade that energy markets would experience a significant shift from relative supply growth to stringency. The reduced rate of discovery and development of domestic crude oil, coupled with import controls on foreign crude supplies, limited the rate of growth of supply of domestic crude oil and subsequently of domestically produced petroleum products. At the same time demands for these products continued to increase at previous high rates, plus or minus a percentage point, given the prevailing favorable business conditions. Furthermore, Nixon administration price controls in 1972 and 1973, specifically

TABLE 1 *Consumer Price Indices (1967 = 100)*

Year	Energy	All other items
1970	107.0	117.0
1971	111.2	122.0
1972	114.3	126.1
1973	123.5	133.8
1974	159.7	146.9
1975	176.6	160.2
1976	189.3	169.2
1977	207.3	179.8
1978	220.4	193.8
1979	275.9	213.1
1980	361.1	238.0

SOURCE: *Economic Report of the President*, February 1982, Table B–54, p. 294.

extended in 1973 and 1974 just to cover petroleum products, increased demands relative to those for other goods and services not under controls. Years of decline in real prices for coal and natural gas resulted in relatively large increases in demands for these fuels. These conditions together brought about increases in consumer demands for all three basic energy resources that exceeded immediate production increases, causing real prices to begin to rise in 1972 and 1973.

The crude oil embargo by Middle East producing countries against the United States in 1973 exacerbated the relative stringency of basic supply from domestic sources. This political action in 1974 both reduced imports into the United States and then substantially increased crude prices worldwide. But while world crude prices went up more than 200 percent, United States crude prices increased only 56 percent because of federal ceilings on domestic products prices. With world crude oil prices roughly constant in real terms over 1975–1978, the controlled domestic prices increased slowly to approximately two-thirds of the world price level. Each increased by roughly 25 and then 50 percent successively in 1979 and 1980. United States crude prices never caught up with, but rather were at 60 percent of international crude prices at the end of the decade.

The crude oil price increases were duplicated only partially by price changes for other fuels. In attempts to shift away from high-priced crude, industrial and commercial consumers increased coal demand and prices, but only very slowly. Substantial increases in natural gas demand were registered in price increases even more slowly, because gas prices were regulated at levels set not by demands but by past historical production costs.[1]

Even so, energy price increases penetrated most sectors of the

1. This argument can be illustrated by the following diagram. With competitive market conditions establishing an equilibrium price p_1 and sales level q_1, regulation is imposed in time period t_2 that holds price at historical costs. The regulated price level when set by historical marginal costs would be p_1, and by historical average costs would be p_2. Supply stays at q_2. But demands have increased from D_1 to D_2. Neither of the regulated price levels then clears the market, with p_1 resulting in excess demands of $(q_2 - q_1)$ and p_2 resulting in $(q_3 - q_1)$. These excess

economy. The costs of manufactured goods increased, particularly of products using large amounts of energy, causing consumer prices to increase. The energy and manufactured-goods components of the price index for the economy as a whole increased substantially in the middle to late 1970s as a result of rising crude prices (as shown in Table 1). Other components also increased as federal credit and money-creation programs sought to prevent the slowdown of these business sectors as more was spent on energy-related goods. Thus energy price increases caused inflation in the index for that component, and may have helped to initiate monetary policies contributing to economywide price inflation.

Various production decisions in the economy were affected in different ways. Investment was redirected toward reducing fuel costs, thereby substituting new equipment for fuel. Exploration and development of fuel sources within the United States increased and there were income as well as output effects. Low-income groups found that they were required to spend proportionately more of their income on energy. But more employment resulted from energy price increases as employers substituted labor for energy in the manufacturing process. Thus the income reductions from energy price increases were at least in part offset by increases in income-earning opportunities from these same price increments.

---

demands are not registered in the market as consumption but are forced into other energy markets.

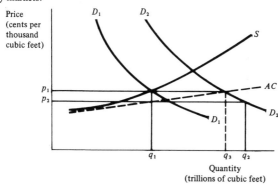

Consumers were affected in other ways as well. Their cutbacks in demand following the 1974 price increases evidenced reduced levels of satisfaction, and this condition was made much worse by the threat of interruptions in fuel supply. There were short periods in 1974 and again in 1979 in which shortages in fuel supplies caused cutbacks in the production of other final goods and services as well. At the time these conditions contributed to increased demands for fuel inventories and reduced demands for other goods, particularly fuel-using consumer durables. Since all this occurred during the first stages of an economywide recession, it is suspected that it contributed to the magnitude of the downturn.

Policy Actions in the 1970s

In retrospect the markets for energy were beset by new supply stringencies of significant dimensions. Discoveries of new reserves had been on the decline for some time, so that production of oil or gas had to decline at prevailing prices. To these conditions were added new stringencies on capital supply for companies distributing gas and electricity. While these reductions in capital were realized not only in the public utilities, but were common to all companies seeking capital in the financial markets, the policy response of the regulatory agencies to them was specific to the energy sector.

The government certainly had available in the mid-1970s all of the traditional tools to respond to these new conditions. It could have taxed consumers to reduce demands in keeping with reduced resource and capital supplies. In the exact opposite policy direction, it could have taxed suppliers so as to increase the rate of response of energy markets to reduced supplies. This would have resulted in prices rising more rapidly, to restrain otherwise increasing demands to levels compatible with the new supply stringency. Such policies could have included tariffs on crude oil imports to raise the supply price of this source, and higher regulated prices for old gas set at levels currently being realized for new supplies.

A third route available for Congress and the Executive Office was to control prices directly. Rather than taxing, price increases could be suppressed at existing quantities. It is the theme of this study that in attempting to control prices in such a way, energy policies of the 1970s exacerbated the new conditions of supply stringency.

This latter route, the one chosen by the federal government, involved various and sundry initiatives. First of all, price controls in place as part of temporary Nixon wage-price ceilings of 1971–1973 were permanently extended to cover all domestic crude and petroleum product prices. These were supplemented to include regulations for the allocation of supplies of petroleum products. In addition, policy initiatives were taken to reduce domestic vulnerability to embargoes and to ease adverse effects on consumers. These included subsidies, use controls, and government operations particularly in fuel storage. But the central element of policy was given over to price regulations for all production and retail deliveries of energy.

These new policies in crude oil and product markets worked one way during equilibrium periods and another way when an unexpected supply stringency caused a short-term disequilibrium. When supply and demand were in balance, efforts to hold down prices for consumers failed as the wellhead price reductions were dissipated by the increased markups at the retail level that were also allowed under the regulations. Thus virtually no price benefit was realized by consumers. Yet these controls did keep the domestic price for crude below world levels, resulting in decreased domestic production and increased reliance on imports. And when there were supply reductions due to import disruptions, these controls reduced the amount of crude available for refining and substantial shortages of gasoline resulted. Attempts to counter shortages caused such shortages.

Natural gas markets had been regulated since the late 1950s at the interstate level, and these price controls resulted in shortages in the 1960s. In view of this experience, the Carter administration sought to establish a schedule of gradual deregulation of natural gas. In passing the Natural Gas Policy Act of 1978 (NGPA), Congress extended controls to intrastate markets and established a complex price schedule for gradual decontrol tied to the anticipated world oil price to 1985. After the unexpected and large crude oil price increases in 1979–1980, the pricing schedule specified by the NGPA was outdated. Given these provisions, prices were thus set below the market clearing level. However, by giving interstate buyers access to intrastate supplies and to some new supplies completely outside of controls, the legislation held off any immediate shortages. This lowered the visibility of any future shortage.

Furthermore, complete decontrol by the NGPA of a limited part of new gas supplies would allow average prices to increase to an equilibrium level. This would take place, at least in theory, by having the old (price-controlled) gas subsidize the new (uncontrolled) supplies. The margin between old and equilibrium prices would be dissipated in gas during the early 1980s, as it was in crude oil by the last half of the 1970s. The new gas and oil policies of the 1970s designed to avoid shortages were to do so by using price-controlled old production to subsidize very-high-cost new or imported supplies.

In the electric power industry, rate-setting practices have not permitted rates or prices to adjust readily to the rising costs inherent in capital stringency. This has had the same effect as oil and gas price controls, first by more intensely exploiting existing stock, and then by slowing down the additions to that stock, but this time in capital rather than in the reserves of a natural resource. By the early 1980s the industry had become deficient in capacity growth and the potential for shortages late in the decade had developed. By keeping a ceiling on prices, those formulating and carrying out these policies hoped to benefit consumers by keeping down final consumption expenditures. But that is not possible when as a consequence supplies are reduced and demands are increased to exacerbate the initial impact of stringency. Nor is it realized when price ceilings at the production stage are not passed through as lower prices to consumers. Both of these faults prevailed.

These results were a product of a particular combination of goals and the available instruments. The goals of these programs were quite straightforward. Whether general or specific to one group of producers or consumers, they were to reduce inflation, eliminate import embargo vulnerability, and ameliorate adverse consumer income effects.

But not all of these could be achieved at once with the policy instruments at hand. Reducing inflation and adverse income effects by freezing domestic energy prices reduces domestic supplies. With less domestic capacity, the demand for imports increases, adding to embargo vulnerability. Thus the first factor of policy evaluation—examining the soundness of policy objectives—shows that, taken as a whole, the energy policies of the 1970s possessed conflicting goals which could not be achieved simultaneously.

Targeted programs may appear to be less contradictory in design and application, but that is an illusion. Price ceilings on one type of fuel to ameliorate adverse effects from higher prices on some group of consumers create incentives to redirect supplies elsewhere, thereby creating shortages for those supposedly advantaged. Subsidy programs to increase conservation or improve environmental quality can be advantageous to a particular group, but even here there can be substantial diversion of goods and services away from the so-called advantaged group. There is no easy way to separate consumers so as to help just some of them.

Thus more domestic energy production, more stable prices, and more equal income distribution compete for priority in any set of energy policies. Even when purposes have been sorted out, the operations put into place to achieve them can still have perverse or partially conflicting results. Whether price controls or production subsidies, the various tools used to achieve certain goals can and do operate at lower levels of effectiveness than expected.

New Legislation in the 1970s

Even given the complexity and possible inconsistency of goals, the government in fact specified certain instruments to be applied in all aspects of the new energy policy. Though not stated directly nor always practiced consistently, the Congress and the White House acted as if price controls were the means for dealing with all the adverse effects of supply stringency and embargoes.

More than half a dozen pieces of major legislation were passed in the 1973–1979 period after years of no such changes (as in Table 2). In addition, numerous important decisions were rendered by the agencies and commissions required to regulate energy industries under the new legislation. In the early and middle 1970s they seem to have centered on price-control methods rather closely. In the late 1970s these regulations gradually disappeared as the economywide efficiency losses from such programs proved to be substantial.

Among these statutes and regulations, six emerged over the decade as the source of energy policy. *The Emergency Petroleum Allocation Act* (EPAA) laid out procedures in 1973 for price and product allocation controls on domestically produced crude oil and on all final sales of petroleum products. These controls were continued by *The Energy Policy and Conservation Act* (EPCA) of 1975, except that price ceilings on newly developed domestic crude oil supplies were made more restrictive and all ceilings were scheduled to be phased out in the early 1980s. *The Natural Gas Policy Act* of 1978 laid out quite specific schedules of price controls on wellhead gas in the United States, again to be partially phased out in the early and middle 1980s. This act fitted in on top of federal regulation of gas pipelines and state public utility regulations of retail gas distribution. Electricity generation was regulated in similar ways. Electricity production was most directly affected by a series of mandatory oil-conservation measures first specified in *The Public Utility Regulatory Policies Act* of 1978 and then extended in *The Powerplant and Industrial Fuel Use Act*. These laws specified the replacement of petroleum products

TABLE 2 *Major Legislative and Administrative Initiatives in Energy Policy*

Act	Year put into effect	Agency	Present status	Provisions
Economic Stabilization Act Amendments PL 93–28, S398	1973	President	Expired	Gave the president discretionary authority to establish priorities of use for allocation of petroleum products and to control prices until April 30, 1974
Emergency Petroleum Allocation Act PL 93–159, S1570	1973	President; later Federal Energy Administration	Expired	Required the president to set up a comprehensive allocation program of crude oil, residual fuel oil, refined petroleum, according to 1972 fuel usage amounts
Energy Policy and Conservation Act PL 94–163, S622	1975	FEA	Expired on presidential order in 1981	Continued price controls on domestic oil until 1979; agency given authority to order major power plants to switch to coal; president authorized to prescribe conservation and gas rationing plans

TABLE 2 *Major Legislative and Administrative Initiatives in Energy Policy (continued)*

Act	Year put into effect	Agency	Present status	Provisions
Public Utility Regulatory Policies Act PL 95–617, HR4018	1978	Federal Energy Regulatory Commission (FERC); Department of Energy (DOE, organized under PL 95–91, S826 in 1977)	In effect	State utility commissions required to consider energy-saving methods in pricing electricity; powerplants required to switch to coal from petroleum and natural gas
National Energy Conservation Policy Act PL 95–619, HR5037	1978	DOE	In effect	Required that gas and electric utilities inform their customers of available energy-savings measures; authorization of funding for weatherization; set conservation policy

TABLE 2 (*continued*)

Powerplant and Industrial Fuel Use Act PL 95–620, HR5146	1978–79	FERC DOE	In effect	Barred new electric power plants and new major fuel-burning installations from natural gas or oil as a primary energy source
Natural Gas Policy Act PL 95–621, HR5289	1978	FERC	In effect	Established a scaled ceiling price for new gas; provided that this price would rise until decontrolled in 1985
Crude Oil Windfall Profits Tax Act PL 96–223, HR3919	1980	DOE	In effect	Imposed an excise tax on crude oil prices to be paid by the producer
Energy Security Act PL 96–294, S932	1980	DOE	In effect	Authorized $20 billion to be allocated to private industry by a Synthetic Fuels Corporation

SOURCE: United States Statutes at Large, 93rd to 96th Congresses.

with coal in the generation of electricity. Thus both the rate of utilization and the particular fuel were to be determined by regulations, at least for some consumers. In addition, federal taxes on the prices of crude oil were imposed by *The Crude Oil Windfall Profits Tax Act* of 1980. This tax was to fill the gap between the controlled wellhead prices and uncontrolled final-products prices as regulations were phased out. Thus price ceilings, quantity limits, and sales taxes covered all aspects of the transactions for petroleum products and most of those for natural gas and electricity.

Statutes alone do not make effective public policy, but are fleshed out by rule making in the regulatory agencies. The petroleum price-control process was set out by the Federal Energy Administration (FEA) in 1974 along lines established by the Cost of Living Council in Nixon's wage-price freeze policies of 1972 and 1973. The process was modified over time by numerous and complicated administrative decisions that while having diverse effects consistently benefited small refining and marketing interests in the products industry. Basically it froze markups on wellhead ceiling crude prices, except for fuel oil, in which an FEA decision was made to eliminate markup controls. At the same time the Federal Power Commission, faced with increasing pressures of excess demand for gas, doubled price ceilings on natural gas at the wellhead. The Department of Energy (DOE) after 1978 increased prices on flowing gas further, and added case-by-case decisions on crude oil conservation requirements and powerplant fuel switching. In contrast to wellhead oil and gas price increases, as many as 100 case decisions each year by state public utility commissions set a pattern of controls over retail gas and electricity prices increasingly resistant to price rises to ameliorate supply reductions.

Together the new statutes and agency operating decisions made over energy policy. They worked in the direction of extending and consolidating price controls, possibly because of the strong consensus of the mid-1970s that something had to be done and that actions taken should first and foremost protect the consumer from price increases.

That viewpoint was manifest in the widely read and quoted 1974 report of the Energy Policy Project of the Ford Foundation, *A Time to Choose.*[2] The report proposed a "technical fix" to reduce the growth of energy consumption to 2 percent a year, less than half the rate realized in periods of full employment and capacity economic growth. Energy demand was to be reduced by mandatory conservation measures, principally revised building codes, usage standards for space-heating equipment, and fuel-economy performance standards for automobiles. At the same time price controls on domestic oil and gas production were to be imposed to protect low-income consumers from fuel price hikes while providing "ample incentives . . . for industry to produce the required quantities of fuel."[3] The "fix" stabilized prices and set out conservation regulations to redistribute income from suppliers to consumers. By curtailing demands and not reducing supplies, the Ford scheme reduced the growth of crude imports. By controlling prices it contained any adverse income effects from sharp price increases following from a supply stringency like that of the mid-1970s.

After the EPAA set out and the EPCA more firmly fixed price controls, the NECA placed the "technical fix" on energy demand. To be sure, there were some contradictions to the "fix" strategy, such as that in phasing out crude oil price controls in the EPCA and that in partially deregulating new gas prices in the Natural Gas Policy Act of 1978. But both acts put in place more elaborate controls in the late 1970s than existed before, and the phasing-out of controls was to be so prolonged that for all intents and purposes the "fix" strategy was established for that decade.

2. S. David Freeman, *A Time to Choose* (Cambridge, Mass.: Ballinger, 1974). Reviews of the Ford Foundation Report appeared in 1974 in *Business Week* (April 6), *Science* (April 12), the *New York Times* (October 18), and *Time* (October 28).

3. Cf. Freeman, pp. 332–33. But a complication arose when supply fell short of demand: then taxes were to be used to increase prices until demand was reduced further.

An Overview of Market Behavior and Policy Results in the 1970s

The question is how well this statute approach worked. There were in fact important changes in production and consumption of energy in the United States resulting from "fix" policies in the last half of the 1970s. Some of the changes were related to new supply-and-demand conditions in markets for crude oil, gas, and other fuels. Others occurred because of the methods used for putting the new regulations into effect. Changes occurred because of unexpected events such as public rejection of nuclear power after the 1979 Three Mile Island plant accident, or the withdrawal of Iran as an important source of supply in the world crude market after the revolution in that country.

Most important, however, were changes in the underlying trends in demand growth and in world crude oil supply. For more than a decade increased incomes and falling prices had brought about substitution of petroleum products for other fuels, to such an extent that growth of products consumption exceeded the annual growth rate of the economy. At the same time the growth of crude supply in the United States slowed down and then ceased altogether, because of reduced resource discovery in the 1960s. Imports grew rapidly to fill these increasing demands. But then prices of these imports in 1972 dollars increased threefold during the 1973–1974 embargo and doubled once again during the supply reductions by Iran and Iraq in 1979 and 1980. With prices for marginal (imported) supplies increasing substantially, domestic crude oil and petroleum products prices had to increase.[4] They brought prices of other fuels up as well, as demands shifted away from the

4. This principle of market behavior is illustrated in the following diagram. With S_D indicative of domestic supply and S_I of the supply of imports at world price (p^*), then supply for domestic refiners is traced out as the lowest portions of these two functions. This is because no domestic refiner will pay more to importers for supplies that are cheaper from domestic sources, or vice versa. With total refiners (and consumers) demand as shown by D, price will tend to gravitate to p^*, the price of that source of supply sufficient to meet all demands. At market clearing sales of q^* million barrels per day, all producers receive p^*.

higher priced crude imports, and substitution of these other fuels took hold, subject in many cases to their own price and distribution regulations.

During the last half of the 1970s petroleum products demand increased, as did that for the production of electricity. Natural gas demands probably increased as well, but utilization declined over this period because of shortages making it impossible to realize demands. The overall rate of energy utilization increased by only 2 percent per year, from 70.7 quadrillion BTUs in 1975 to 79.0 quadrillion BTUs in 1979 (as in Table 3). As the decade ended, utilization rates for 1980 showed substantial declines compared to 1979, as the slowdown of the economy and price increases both worked against maintaining the earlier 2 percent rate of growth.

This sharp reduction in the rate of demand growth is remarkably close to that predicted to follow from the "technical fix" strategy. Indeed the realized rate of growth of demand for the 1975–1980 period is virtually identical to that "technical fix" rate of growth necessary to arrive at the 1985 forecast level. From this base, if the economy were to proceed through recovery to full-employment GNP growth in the early 1980s, energy demand growth at one-half of GNP growth would result in total energy use of 86 quadrillion BTUs in 1985, exactly as forecast in the "technical fix" scenario.

That would be a remarkable coincidence. Even though total

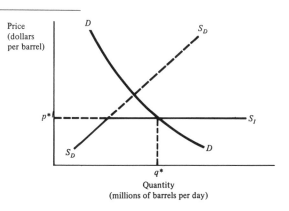

TABLE 3 *Composition of United States Energy Utilization, 1970–1979*

Year	Petroleum[a] (%)	Natural gas (%)	Nuclear (%)	Coal[b] (%)	Total energy consumption (quadrillion BTUs)
1970	44.2	32.6	0.4	18.9	66.8
1975	46.3	28.2	2.7	18.1	70.7
1979	47.0	26.2	3.5	19.1	79.0

[a]Refined petroleum products including natural gas plant liquids and crude oil burned as fuel.

[b]Bituminous, lignite, and anthracite coal.

SOURCE: Department of Energy/Energy Information Administration, *Annual Report to Congress 1980*, Vol. 2, p. 7.

consumption is similar to the "fix" forecast, there have been substantial differences between prices and quantities for each fuel expected from the "fix" policy and those realized from the new legislation actually put into effect. Fuel switching out of petroleum products mandated by the "fix" regulations did not take place. Regulations setting energy-efficient standards in building construction were never made effective. Most important, price increases were in fact substantially greater than those expected to occur under the "fix" policy. The "technical fix" for reducing demand at constant prices was not realized, but rather was replaced by nonpolicy price increases substantially greater than the general inflation rate throughout this part of the decade (as shown in Table 4). Because prices rose much more than forecast, particularly for crude oil and petroleum products, there were considerable reductions in quantities demanded, indeed to levels consistent with the operations of controls on consumption in the "fix" strategy.[5]

5. The way in which the market operated to produce the "fix" result can be illustrated with an extension of the diagram given in footnote 4. Here $S_I S_I$ repro-

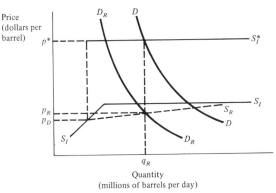

duces the supply function of domestic production and imports, as forecast by the Ford Foundation Report for conditions of no price controls. The "fix" results in supply S_R in which regulated p_D is arranged with imported price consistent with S_I. With demand reduced to D_R by conservation policies, markets clear at q_R. But world crude prices increase much more than forecast, to the level p^*, and neither domestic price nor conservation controls have their intended effects. Thus markets clear at q_R and price p^* rather than at price p_R.

TABLE 4 *United States Energy Prices, 1980–1985*

	1980		1985 predicted[a]	
	Index	Annual % change from 1975	Index	Annual % change from 1975
Coal				
Actual	467	3.88	—	—
Predicted	429	2.13	477	2.13
Crude petroleum				
Actual	552	17.54	**[b]	—
Predicted	297	3.85	359	3.85
Electricity				
Actual	332	10.78	**[b]	—
Predicted	239	4.33	295	4.33
Gas				
Actual	761	28.52	**[b]	—
Predicted	292	6.12	393	6.12
GNP Deflator				
Actual	177.4	6.88	—	—
Predicted	153.4	3.82	185	3.82

[a] Predictions are taken from Table F–3 ("Technical fix growth") of the Ford Foundation Report (David S. Freeman, *A Time to Choose* [Cambridge, Mass.: Ballinger, 1974]), p. 503.

[b] Indicates that the prediction for 1985 price has already been exceeded by actual 1980 prices.

SOURCES: U.S. Bureau of Labor Statistics, *Producer Prices and Price Indexes*, monthly and annual; Bureau of Economic Analysis, *Survey of Current Business*, July issues, March 1980, and March 1981.

Fuel share predictions were not realized, by coincidence or otherwise. Petroleum products continued to grow as a percentage of total consumption. One reason was that requirements to switch from petroleum to coal were not put into effect generally and immediately because of limits on coal burning from environmental protection policies, but principally because of disincentives for investments required to make the fuel switch under public utility rate-making procedures. Another reason was that a significant and pervasive natural gas shortage developed in the 1974–1978 period that curtailed switching from fuel oil to gas in commercial and industrial operations. Nuclear powerplant construction slowdowns and cancellations caused by new safety requirements and cost increases prevented substitution of nuclear for fossil fuels. Thus a combination of unexpected large price increases working on the demand side, and increased resistance to policies favoring substitution for crude oil on the supply side, produced a smaller energy market basket more centered on petroleum products.

How did these policies work in pursuing their objectives of efficiency, income redistribution, and reducing embargo vulnerability? Controls on wellhead prices for domestic production under the EPAA and EPCA as administered by the FEA and DOE resulted in substantially lower domestic wellhead price levels. The imported crude oil price increases following from the world supply reductions in 1974 and 1979 were not passed through at once to domestic consumers, but rather were averaged with the lower prices on domestic regulated supply. But by the late 1970s consumers were paying the same prices in this country as elsewhere because the lower crude regulated price was offset in final product prices by higher refining and marketing costs. The operating regulations themselves may have caused part of these higher costs. Since Federal Energy Administration regulations setting limits on refinery markups made no allowance for recovery of refinery capital costs, operating costs of old refineries increased as their operations were extended. Marketing costs were increased as the allocation system became frozen in place. In addition, marketing markups of prices over costs increased as the FEA and successively the DOE allowed higher margins in response to applications of retailers in case proceedings. Altogether, politics worked to fill in the gap between world and domestic crude prices with regulating costs and entitlements.[6]

In addition, the "entitlements" program giving each refiner access to the price-controlled old domestic crude worked in practice to give more lower priced crude to smaller refiners. Joseph Kalt found the entitlements program to be a "mechanism by which property rights are established for price-controlled domestic crude oil."[7] The property right, worth the difference between the domestic controlled and the imported uncontrolled crude price, was a source of returns to refiners totalling $14–$15 billion per year after 1974, an amount making up roughly 60 percent of the total import-domestic crude purchase cost difference. Such returns were income lost by consumers from the regulatory process.[8]

Beyond such effects on producers, the "fix" policy appears to have contributed to another supply result. By holding wellhead prices below those for imports, the policy reduced domestic supplies and replaced them with crude from abroad. This substitution of a domestic barrel of crude not available at ceiling prices for one at world prices had its costs, given that the resources required to obtain the imports were greater.[9]

The goal of consumer protection against price increases was not achieved. Refined products price controls were not binding and therefore had no such protective effect, except during the two import supply interruptions of 1974 and 1979. Moreover, by controlling prices while supplies decreased, and particularly by reallocating the remaining short supplies so as to reduce them further,

6. These effects are analyzed and assessed in the next chapter.

7. Joseph Kalt, *The Economics and Politics of Oil Price Regulation* (Cambridge, Mass.: Massachusetts Institute of Technology Press, 1981), p. 64.

8. This was the case because a substantial portion was reallocated from large to small refiners. Thus intramarginal suppliers had lower costs. The cost differences were transformed into refiner rents rather than price reductions because they did not accrue to the marginal sources of supply that determined prices.

9. This can be illustrated with the previous diagram. Given that wellhead regulation keeps domestic crude prices under a ceiling of p_R, domestic production is

the FEA and DOE in part created those shortages.[10] This was accomplished by obstructing the allocative effects of price increases and by sequestering supplies for users that took them off the market. The reactions to these programs included increased building of inventories of both energy supplies and final products. The hoarding of materials caused slowdowns of production and reductions in investment.

While not exactly measurable, these reactions have been given credit in part for the 1974–1975 recession and the slowdown of the economy again in 1980. Such attribution probably goes too far, however. Even though such price policies had an inventory-building effect, it is not possible to argue successfully that they caused the two recessions of the 1970s. Both the 1974 and 1979 petroleum shortages occurred when there was widespread expectation of an economywide slowdown in GNP growth, as a recurrent phase of the business cycle and as a result of both the Nixon and Carter administrations' monetary and fiscal restraints. The energy price increases alone probably added less than two per-

---

reduced by $q_D - q_R$. These have to be replaced by imports, since total consumption stays at q^* whether or not there is domestic price control (since the vertical dis-

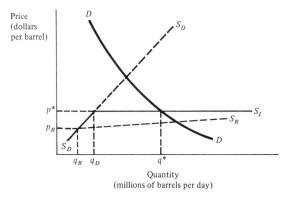

tance by supply under regulated wellhead price S_R and market supply S_I is filled up with the costs and entitlements of regulation).

10. This result is dealt with at great length in the next chapter.

centage points to consumer price inflation. They may have contributed to but did not by themselves cause the sharp reductions in investment that characterized the two recessions. Although "large and unanticipated changes in the price of energy are found to have substantial disruptive effects on the economy," as Hall and Mork indicate, "other forces were present such as the removal of the general price controls of the Economic Stabilization Program and the slowdown of investment activity after the preceding mini boom."[11]

The Overall Effects

The impact of the new policies came from keeping crude prices down while limiting utilization of other fuels. Even though consumers eventually paid the full petroleum products price, this control of substitutions had to increase the consumption of petroleum products. And by constraining prices of domestically produced crude, the development and extraction of local supply from in-ground reserves were reduced so that the increased utilization came from additional imports. By 1979, with world prices in real terms one-third higher than the average controlled domestic wellhead price, the displacement appears to have become quite substantial. United States demands with controls were at least a million barrels more than would have been realized without controls.[12]

These conditions in turn adversely affected energy production, general inflation, and economywide growth. The crude oil shortage periods coincided with and may have contributed to the recessions of 1974 and 1979–1980. The size of this effect has not been

11. Robert Hall and Knut A. Mork, "Energy Prices, Inflation, and Recession, 1974–1975," *Energy Journal* 1, no. 3 (July 1980): 54. See also Otto Eckstein, *The Great Recession, with a Postscript on Stagflation* (Amsterdam: North-Holland; New York: American Elsevier, 1978); and Richard Gordon, *U.S. Coal and the Electric Power Industry* (Baltimore: Johns Hopkins University Press, for Resources for the Future, 1975).

12. Such an estimate is explained and documented in the last section of the next chapter.

determined, however, and indeed recessions are caused by so many factors that perhaps no causal relations could be established. But further, it is reasonable to conclude that the shortage conditions had adverse effects on consumers supposedly protected by the regulations.

There are similar results from the "fix" on the choice of fuel. Gas controls created shortages of that fuel, not to be ameliorated by the Natural Gas Policy Act of 1978.[13] Replacing oil with gas was limited because of that condition. Mandated fuel switching should have led to widespread replacements of oil with coal. But fuel switching was deferred where other regulations conflicted,[14] and thus few plants were converted on time schedules in keeping with a reduced petroleum share of all energy consumption in the early 1980s. There were more exceptions than there were applications of the switching rule, so that the "fix" was not an operating regulatory process.

Thus controlling prices had adverse energy security effects. Not only were price controls not effective at the consumer level as planned, but at the crude level they had undesired consequences for the costs for supplies. They reduced allocative efficiency of fuels among consumers. The mistake was in assuming little or no policy effect on domestic supply of any of these fuels. The second mistake was in expecting the consumer to be better off as a result of substantial conservation when conservation policy was not practiced. Failing to reduce demands in the crude market by decree, the strategy had to produce shortages when there were sharp import and domestic supply reductions of one fuel or the other. The mistakes could only lead to a larger share of energy consumption for imports, the most insecure fuel source. The lesson of the 1970s was that price-control responses to supply scarcity worsened market conditions for all concerned.

The implications from this lesson for policy in the 1980s have to be drawn out in some detail from the particular experience in crude oil, natural gas, and electricity. This is the subject of the

13. These conditions are described in detail in Chapter 3.
14. These other regulations are the topic of Chapter 4.

next three chapters, with crude and petroleum products behavior analyzed in Chapter 2, natural gas at the wellhead in Chapter 3 and at retail in Chapter 4, and electricity in production and retail also in Chapter 4. The prospects for these and alternative policies are dealt with in the last chapter.

2

◇◇◇◇◇

Policy on Petroleum Products Pricing

THE FOCUS OF energy policy in the 1970s was squarely on the prices of gasoline and fuel oil. These fuels were used throughout the economy, and controls on their prices would have both the equity and anticyclical effects. The general results of controls were quite the opposite, however, from those expected. The details of these price regulations are worth examining to find an explanation for this difference. Moreover the results have not disappeared even though the control apparatus was dismantled in 1981. The "windfall taxes" put in their place have had the same effects and are likely to dominate the results from energy policy in the 1980s.

The First Steps Toward Price Control

Although the Nixon wage-price controls of the early 1970s were new in content and scope for the oil industry, they were not the first ever imposed on that industry. Regulatory programs designed to stabilize domestic petroleum prices had been in effect since the 1930s. During the middle 1930s the major producing states in the Southwest operated an interstate compact to restrict supply to levels below the maximum efficient rate of production from reserves of crude oil. Under this "prorationing" program, the state agencies collectively set production at levels below what would have been competitive supply given production conditions at that time.

This collective state regulation was buttressed by federal enforcement of laws prohibiting shipments of petroleum in excess of the allocations across state lines under the Connolly Hot Oil Act.[1]

Such price-stabilizing schemes worked to the benefit of domestic producers until the middle 1950s, when increased availability of lower cost foreign crude threatened to overwhelm domestic markets with a flood of imports. Concern for domestic producers and for the national security implications of reduced domestic production capacity prompted the Eisenhower administration to establish the Mandatory Oil Import Program in 1959. The MOIP set volumetric limits on imports of crude oil and oil products into the United States; the result was that the marginal barrel of crude that would set refinery purchase prices had to come from domestic sources not subject to limits.

But with steady depletion of domestic production capacity, both prorationing and the MOIP began to unravel in the early 1970s. The state agencies by 1974 set proration allowables at 100 percent of the maximum efficient rate, thereby eliminating any constraints on the operations of particular wells and fields. The MOIP abandoned fixed import levels in 1973, replacing these controls with tariffs. Thus the marginal source of supply consisted of crude imports, and the domestic price level was determined by the world price for exports from the Middle East.[2]

1. Cf. 49 U.S. Statutes 30 (1935).
2. This significant change can be illustrated by the accompanying diagram, based

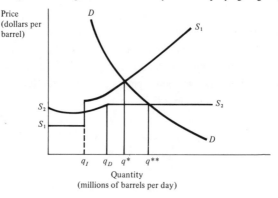

Petroleum Products Regulations in the Nixon Price- and Wage-Control Program

In August 1971 the Nixon administration placed ceilings on prices and wages of all manufactured and traded goods and services. The Phase I freeze of the Economic Stabilization Program ended in November of that year, based on the presumption that inflationary expectations had been broken, to be followed by Phase II providing for only 3 percent annual price increases throughout the economy. The petroleum industry was covered under both Phase I and II controls. Prices were kept down at wholesale and retail, but by means of a clumsy process. The ceilings gave inadequate consideration to seasonal price changes and could not respond flexibly to changing demands, such as during periods of extraordinarily bad weather or of rapid changes in the business cycle.

In January 1973 Phase III was put into effect. Ceilings in this phase were voluntary, and not closely adhered to, so that products prices rose sharply, particularly for propane and home heating oil in the Northeast. At the same time, world crude prices were increasing, because of the large increases in worldwide demands relative to supply as business conditions improved. These conditions brought forth Special Rule One promulgated by the Cost of Living Council under the Phase III program, which reimposed mandatory controls on the twenty-four largest refining companies in the petroleum industry accounting for 95 percent of domestic sales. The results this time were quite predictable. Under Rule One, the suppliers of petroleum products not covered by the controls increased prices at retail and bid up prices of crude oil. With two sets of prices, one for the independents and the other for the

---

on those used in Chapter 1 footnotes. Demands for crude for refining for United States consumers is shown as DD. The supply S_1 is for pre-1970 conditions of strict limits on imports (equal to q_I) and domestic production ($q^* - q_I$). In contrast, supply S_2 is illustrative of the results of the breakdown of prorationing and import-control policies. Domestic costs fall after prorating ends, so that the domestic portion of S_2 lies below S_1. Even so, imports rise when limits are taken off, to ($q^{**} - q_D$).

twenty-four regulated firms, supplies at one location quickly ran out while expensive supplies elsewhere were taken by consumers much more slowly.

An entirely new set of regulations was set out in Phase IV of the program in the summer of 1973 to correct the runs on cheap supplies endemic in the two-price system. These regulations established at the wellhead a two-"tier" pricing system which paid more for crude from newly developed wells than for that from wells on earlier operating properties, in expectation that higher uncontrolled prices would provide incentives for additional supply from newer sources. Refiners were allowed to "roll in" or average these prices as feedstock costs, and were required to limit refinery margins to amounts necessary only to recover refining operating costs. The pass-through of operating costs to specific fuels such as gasoline, home heating oil, or automobile diesel fuel was to be made on the basis of the relative volumes of each product sold into the marketing and retailing system.

Even with these changes there was enough difference in the mix of "old" and "new" crude in each refinery to cause wide variations in regulated product prices. There were continuing shortages of low-priced crude, and of product supplies produced from this crude, during the second and third quarters of 1973. These shortages were sufficiently disruptive to bring forth increased pressures for price increases for "low crude cost" refiners and marketers, or for allocation of the low-cost feedstock in equal refinery shares by government decree. Although steps were taken to do both, uniform crude purchase costs were not established across refineries before 1973.

The Emergency Petroleum Allocation Act of 1973

The catalyst for further policy was the Arab countries' embargo of crude and product shipments to the United States and select other consuming nations in October 1973. While the embargo was actually in operation, the Congress passed a comprehensive program of price controls and rationing for both crude oil and petroleum products. The controls on crude were an extended version of those in Phase IV, involving a system of specified ceilings on "old" production from wells in operation in 1972, but an exemption from ceilings for "new" production from later wells. The new production was to be exempt from control, as was that from "stripper" wells producing less than ten barrels per day. In addition, for every barrel of new oil produced, one barrel of old oil would be released from price controls. The old domestic supplies were placed under ceilings that were designed to be stringent, and in fact the first round of such ceiling prices were much below those in the spot and contract markets for foreign crude at that time.

The most ambitious step taken in the EPAA was allocating crude and products among companies and refineries. A "buyer-seller freeze" program was put into effect that froze crude dispersements into the same trade flows as actually realized in 1972. In the buy / sell program, those refineries short of feedstock were allotted crude from others with higher than average capacity utilization. And from there the disparities in regulated prices were to be eliminated by a program of "entitlements" put into operation late in 1974. Refiners with less than the national average proportion of old to new crude could gain an "entitlement" to more old crude, to be purchased from other refiners at the controlled price. This was designed to put feedstock costs of all the refiners at the same level, given that each would have the national average ratio of old to new crude in its refinery runs.

Price controls were extended to cover all petroleum products as well. Base prices were set at May 15, 1973, levels and any further increases were to be justified by cost increases. The acceptable cost increases included those in average crude or average operating costs. Any allowable price increase not taken could be "banked" for recapture at a later date when market conditions allowed. But increased capital and interest costs were not to be allowed to pass through to product price increases.

There were almost endless exceptions to these rules, with small refiners allowed additional entitlements and importers receiving a proportion of an entitlement for each barrel of certain refined products they brought into the country. There were hardship entitlements, and those defined under an exceptions and appeals process that further eroded the program. Even so, the EPAA established a consistent multitiered system of crude oil price controls that resulted in comprehensive price ceilings for petroleum products. Producers were required to charge less for old domestic crude supplies, and refiners-marketers given equal feedstock costs were required to set the same final prices that were also to be lower than unregulated products prices.[3] The act institutionalized price and distribution controls on refined products throughout the petroleum industry.

The Energy Policy and Conservation Act

In December 1975 the federal regulatory structure was further developed by new statute authority not only to renew the EPAA

3. The intentions of the controls can be illustrated with the diagram from the previous chapter. Domestic demands for crude are shown as DD, and supply is shown as S_1S_1, a combination of domestic supply q_D and imports ($q^* - q_D$). If a

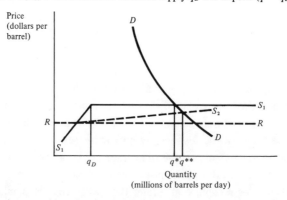

Price
(dollars per barrel)

Quantity
(millions of barrels per day)

ceiling is put on domestic prices at level R, and the lower priced domestic supply is mixed with imports, then the supply curve becomes the curve S_1S_2. The regulated market clears with additional imports ($q^{**} - q^*$), at a price below the import price indicated by the level of the horizontal section of S_1S_1.

but also to extend controls to sources of supply not covered by the earlier act. The focus of this new Energy Policy and Conservation Act (EPCA) was on adding further "tiers" of crude oil wellhead prices, so that ceilings encompassed more of the domestic new crude left uncontrolled by the EPAA. But while present controls were to be more complete, the EPCA set out a program for reducing all controls of refined products prices gradually over the forthcoming few years. Where the regulatory agency could show sufficiency of supply and of competition in some product, price controls were to be allowed to be eliminated on that product. In fact the Federal Energy Administration proposed and completed removal of price ceilings on residual fuel, home heating fuel, and some types of jet fuel along with various specialty products within two years of passage of the EPCA. Thus controls in the late 1970s were centered on prices and allocations of crude oil, and on selected final products that included gasoline, propane natural gas liquids, and other aviation fuels.

The Purpose and Structure of FEA Regulation

Under these pieces of legislation the Federal Energy Administration was given broad and weighty responsibilities in the conduct of regulation. The FEA was charged with conducting a price and allocation control program for "protection of public health" and the "maintenance of public services." More central to the agency's mandate was the "preservation of an economically sound and competitive petroleum industry" and "the maintenance of, exploration for and production or extraction of fuels and minerals essential to the requirements of the United States" [cf. EPAA, section 4(B) (1)]. But the FEA was also called upon to allocate crude oil to refineries so as to permit "such refineries to operate at full capacity" and to allocate refined petroleum products "at equitable prices among all regions and areas of the United States and sectors of the petroleum industry." This was to be done while achieving "economic efficiency and the minimization of economic distortion, inflexibility and unnecessary interference with market mechanisms.'' With such an array of goals, the agency could only fall short of full attainment.

Even so, the congressional policies of the late 1970s were based on the assumption that a program centered on crude oil price controls would come closest to the mark on all these initiatives. By keeping domestic crude prices below world levels, the adverse effects of arbitrary OPEC price hikes could be avoided, including those on the real incomes of small consumers and those from inflation throughout the economy.[4] This could be done without interfering with competition or substantially reducing the supply of new crude. The market under price ceilings would approximately balance, even if not perfectly, and would operate efficiently.[5]

Section 8A of the EPAA, as amended by the EPCA, required

4. For congressional expression of these goals, see House Report 94–340, 94th Cong., 1st sess. (1975), pp. 7–9.

5. The critical assumptions establishing price controls are the elasticities of supply and demand. If both are quite inelastic, as illustrated, then prices can be reduced

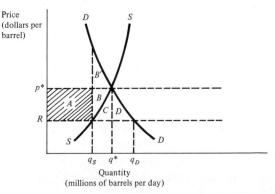

from p^* without regulation to R with regulation. The equity gains are indicated by area A, as reductions in expenditures for the established rate of consumption. To be sure, production $(q^* - q_S)$ is lost, and thus efficiency is reduced (since this is output for which consumers are willing to pay). Also, demand is artificially increased by the reduced price, by $(q_D - q^*)$, and excess demand is thus increased by $(q_D - q_S)$. Those not receiving supply lose $B'BCD$, for which they would pay BCD. But these losses are small, given highly inelastic supply and demand curves.

the Federal Energy Administration to establish a crude oil pricing structure which would result in the average national price for all domestically produced crude to be set at $7.66 per barrel. This price level was to be adjusted upward by the FEA at a rate up to 10 percent annually to compensate for the effects of inflation but further increases could only be authorized over the potential veto of Congress. Pricing structure regulations also were set out, in this case not only to hold down the price level but also to specify that owners of lower cost "old" crude would not receive windfalls as the domestic market price increased toward the new, higher world price levels. But marginal or "new" crude was permitted to approximate world prices more closely, based on the premise that costs of these supplies would approach the import price level as they expanded to replace imports.

The FEA established in early 1976 a functioning three-"tier" system of crude pricing.[6] The first tier consisted of a price ceiling on old oil from established fields operating at 1975 production rates. The second tier was a price ceiling for "new" oil defined as that in excess of production from established properties in the 1975 base year. The third was composed of unregulated prices, such as for imported oil, oil from stripper wells, and in 1979–1980 for heavy oil along with oil from newly discovered or developed properties. The resulting price structure is shown in Table 5, with first-tier prices ranging between $5.00 and $6.00 per barrel, and second-tier prices ranging between $11.00 and $14.00 per barrel. As indicated by stripper prices, the range for unregulated or third-tier prices was in fact from $12.00 to $36.00 a barrel during this five-year period.

The program also attempted to prevent domestic product prices from rising to world levels. The regulations were to prevent marketers from increasing their markups on crude beyond "cost-based" levels, even if this involved keeping prices too low to attract supplies of foreign products into the domestic market. These regulations were quite complex and exceedingly specific, but

6. Cf. 10 Code of Federal Regulations, sections 212.72–77.

TABLE 5   *Regulated Crude Oil Prices, 1976–1980 ($ per barrel)*

Year	Lower tier	Upper tier	Stripper	Alaskan North Slope	Naval petroleum reserve	Average
1976 (Feb.–Dec.)	5.14	11.57	12.17	—	—	8.14
1977	5.19	11.22	13.59	6.35	12.34	8.57
1978	5.46	12.15	13.95	5.22	12.96	9.00
1979	5.95	13.20	22.93	10.57	19.40	12.64
1980 (Jan.–Mar.)	6.32	13.96	36.16	13.77	32.79	18.68

SOURCE: Joseph Kalt, *The Economics and Politics of Oil Price Regulation* (Cambridge, Mass.: Massachusetts Institute of Technology Press, 1980), p. 18; as from DOE / EIA, *Monthly Energy Review*.

essentially set product price at May 15, 1973, levels plus the allowable cost increase. The allowable included any wellhead crude price increases in keeping with the crude price regulations, and increased operating costs, depreciation, maintenance, and severance taxes. As has been mentioned, this limitation created the anomaly of excluding the interest and stockholders' returns necessary to obtain capital.

As crude and product price controls were put into operation, parallel tax policies were developed under the Crude Oil Windfall Profits Tax Act of 1980 to have similar effects. This act sought to remove producer and landowner returns or "windfalls" defined as the difference between EPCA controlled and uncontrolled crude prices. A number of categories of crude were set out, each with its own tax, but essentially 70 percent of the difference between the controlled and uncontrolled prices was removed by this levy. The exception was a new third tier of production, which included output from post-1978 discoveries and from tertiary (high-technology) drilling, to be taxed only at a 30 percent rate. The new tax policy went into operation early in 1980 with the expectation that it would run throughout the decade.

Federal Energy Administration Operations and Gasoline Shortages

During the early stages of the Arab oil embargo of 1973 the Federal Energy Office went into operation under a congressional mandate to "deal with energy shortages, develop energy conservation, and promote efficiencies in the use of energy resources." [7] The FEO managed this country's response to the embargo with consequent effects on petroleum production and consumption until it was replaced by the Federal Energy Administration in June 1974. The FEA became the DOE in 1978 and had its turn to administer regulations during cutbacks in crude supply in 1979, when Iranian

7. U.S. Senate, *Hearings Before the Subcommittee on Government Operations*, December 1973.

production was withdrawn from world markets. Both agencies operated during emergency conditions by setting out rules much the same as those of the state public utility regulatory commissions. The results were to increase the problems already inherent in market institutions in adjusting to lower crude supplies.[8]

8. The process of creation of a shortage is as follows. A disruption in world oil supplies can be represented by a leftward shift in the world supply curve of oil. Such a shift can result from either a loss of reserves or a reduction in production by one or more of the producing countries. This immediate loss of supply forces producing companies to replace supplies by buying on the spot market. The rush on the spot market leads to immediate price increases on spot crude. We see from the figure that the reduction in supply should cause the new equilibrium of official

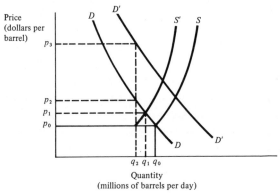

Quantity
(millions of barrels per day)

prices to rise from p_0 to p_1. However, in reality, while there is an increase in the value of crude oil, the price of oil sold by producers to refiners and by refiners to consumers remains at p_0. Data from the period of the Iranian crisis reveal that the official price of crude oil does not initially rise to p_1. Instead the prices set by OPEC slowly adjusted to the spot market. The lag in the adjustment of OPEC prices is an important consideration, for it creates a spread between official prices and spot market prices. This spread makes it profitable for oil companies to build inventories. Since the price paid by most purchasers remains at p_0, there is initially a shortage in the market equal to the difference between q_0 and q_1.

In an unregulated market, supplies eventually raise the price of crude oil sold to consumers to p_1. This allows them to capture the profits created by the lag, and also eliminates the shortage, as the new equilibrium moves to p_1q_1. In a regulated environment, price is not allowed to rise to p_1. This in effect perpetuates the shortage of $(q_0 - q_1)$. It may even be that the shortage is greater. If the buyers of crude oil hold onto part of their supply as prices adjust, and cause the spot value to rise to p_2, the shortage created would equal $(q_0 - q_2)$. This situation occurs if producers of crude oil are unable to raise prices but are able to increase their inventories. Such an action magnifies the disruption.

From October 1973 to June 1974 the market had to adjust to a two- to three-million-barrel-per-day reduction in crude oil and products imports, constituting 30–40 percent of imports and 15–20 percent of total demands. The FEO could have imposed regulatory measures to reduce demands such as increased sales taxes in established markets or it could have controlled prices and then rationed any shortages. The choice depended in part on the size of the supply reduction, with a large reduction likely to have required an administratively difficult rationing scheme under price controls. But there were indications as early as November and December of 1973 that the Saudi Arabian selective boycott against the U.S. was not working, because supplies meant for other consuming countries were being diverted to the East Coast of the United States. Instead of cutting off just United States supplies, the boycott was reducing world supplies evenly and by a relatively small volume. Thus the stage was set for mandating price ceilings and just letting a small proportion of consumers do without.

The cutback was having an effect on world prices, however. The world crude price increases exceeded 50 percent at the time that ceilings were being imposed by regulation on domestic crude prices. Using the 1973 control mechanisms derived by Nixon's Cost of Living Council for all goods and services, the FEO laid out price controls for just domestic crude oil production and refined products. This new energy office required allocations of refinery runs among products, and put into operation regulations that allocated crude among refineries. These had substantial effects in the early months of 1974. In fact they produced substantial shortages, without providing a rationing scheme to determine a fair allocation of the shortfall.

Similarly, consumer response to the difference between spot values and official prices is to increase their stocks, which can be shown by an outward shift of the demand curve to D'. While the initial response of consumers to the shock of rising prices may be to conserve, the expectational response, seeing an increase in spot values, is to stockpile. The shift in the demand curve creates a larger shortage and drives the price even higher, to p_3.

The first round of FEO emergency regulations resulted in a price distribution during 1973 and 1974 in which two-thirds of domestic crude oil supplies were to be sold at $5.25 per barrel with the remaining one-third at $10.00 per barrel. Further, incentives for production from the low-priced sources were offered in the "released oil" provisions, which permitted one barrel of $5.25 oil to be decontrolled for every barrel of $10.00 oil produced. Even so, the regulations provided general disincentives for crude production. Old crude was depleted at an annual rate of 5–15 percent, with ultimate recovery of less than half of any in-ground reserve, because of reduced prices relative to new crude. The losses in production in 1973, as estimated from an equation in the M.I.T. econometric gas and oil model,[9] were 0.33 million barrels per day. Similarly, domestic crude production levels in 1974 would have been 0.25 million barrels per day more if there had not been old oil price controls.

9. The econometric model is described in detail in Paul W. MacAvoy and Robert S. Pindyck, *The Economics of the Natural Gas Shortage (1960–1980)* (Amsterdam: North-Holland; New York American Elsevier 1975). A large-scale model, it focuses both on the political-technical institutions and on economic analysis of the performance of the natural gas industry. Separate equations are estimated by use of generalized least squares (GLS) for (1) exploration and discovery of oil and gas, (2) production of gas out of reserves, (3) pipeline markups, and (4) wholesale demands. While not explicitly dealt with in the M.I.T. model, an oil production equation has recently been estimated with the following results (t-statistics are in parentheses):

$$USQO = 14,432.40 + 9461.71 \ (USPO_t) + 0.08 \ (RSVS_{t-1})$$
$$(2.17) \qquad\qquad (1.75) \qquad\qquad (27.32)$$

$$R^2 = .87 \qquad N = 160 \qquad F = 534.49$$

where $USQO_t$ = quantity of oil produced over twenty U.S. production regions in period t; $USPO_t$ = average U.S. wellhead price of oil in period t; $RSVS_{t-1}$ = total reserves of oil in the previous period.

The above coefficients along with the GLS ρ values for twenty production districts were used to simulate the amount of production that would be forthcoming under regulated and unregulated price policies. The resulting estimate of 0.25–0.33 million barrels per day may be high: the *Oil and Gas Journal,* an industry publication, indicated early in February 1975 that the maximum available from secondary recovery on old fields would be 0.2 million barrels per day.

The regulatory allocations of crude among refineries had an even more important effect. Soon after its formation the Federal Energy Office devised a mechanism to make crude available to refiners heavily dependent on Middle East oil. This was combined with a program to assure supply for refiners that purchased crude from other refining companies in a mandatory interrefinery allocation program by which ''crude-rich'' refiners shared stocks with ''crude-poor'' refiners. The program was put into effect in February 1974 and subsequently revised a number of times to require that refiners with above-average crude supplies sold to others until each operated at the same level of capacity utilization.

But this input averaging was at least a theoretical disincentive to import foreign crude. Any company that imported to utilize its own refining capacity had to pay $10.00 per barrel, but then deliver part of that barrel to other refineries for slightly more than $5.00 per barrel if they were able to obtain enough imports to run at more than the industry average percent of capacity utilization. At best, the imports were placed in a lottery with the purchaser the winner only if below average utilization.

By mid-February of 1974 the FEO had begun to receive indications that the allocation program was indeed curtailing imports by the crude-rich refiners. The Gulf Oil Corporation filed suit against the regulator charging that its order to sell 11.9 million barrels to other refiners was confiscatory. Many other crude-rich refiners complained of the resale price squeeze, as more than 56 million barrels was supplied by importers to crude-poor refiners during the period from February to April. FEO administrator William Simon conceded that the program would lower imports to the East Coast, especially from Venezuela. Deputy Administrator John Sawhill admitted that FEO was considering amendments to the plan, particularly by restricting the size of required deliveries from the crude-rich refiners so as to provide assistance only to ''smaller'' crude-poor refiners.[10]

10. The industry response also involved resistance to these rules. The vague wording in successive revisions of the original order allowed manifold interpretations of what should be the resale price on buy-sell orders. One revision allowed

The restrictive effects on imports from these rules began to appear almost at once. Simon predicted in February 1974 that there would be a decrease in crude imports, and as shown in Table 6, there were indeed reductions in the months in which the allocation program was in effect. By working around the embargo, importers managed to obtain 87 percent of previous months' volumes in November and December. Of course some part of this success derived from having inventories on the high seas shipped before the embargo was imposed, but more came from evading the boycott of shipments to the United States by diverting shipments on the high seas from other consuming countries to domestic refineries. By January when the refinery allocation program was expected to go into effect, imports fell somewhat, and in February and March when the program was in full operation, imports fell considerably. In the first three months of 1974 monthly average imports fell to 73 percent of volumes during the preceding two months.[11]

At that point the situation improved, in part because the regulations were revised to limit the windfalls from buy-sell requirements to the smaller refiners and to those imports within "projected levels." During the period from April to June of 1974 there was a substantial increase in the amount of imports, almost 60 percent more than the amount in the January to March period. The effects are apparent. Administrator Simon had predicted that

"an additional cost" of 84¢ per barrel on every barrel transferred from one refiner to another. A second allowed prices to increase to "reflect crude oil costs prior to making crude oil sales." The word "costs" could be interpreted in a way that allowed sellers to recover completely the original purchase price on the marginal supplies from abroad. Later in the year, Sawhill—now the FEO administrator— complained that those taking advantage of both adjustments were "double dipping" so as to obtain a profit margin of 84¢ per barrel on the $9.87 marginal price of foreign crude oil, and that this had cost the consumers millions of dollars in overcharges. Most companies denied that they had dipped twice, but the possibility existed that there were loopholes allowing evasion of the rules. Cf. U.S. General Accounting Office, "Problems in the Federal Energy Administration's Compliance and Enforcement Effort," December 6, 1974.

11. Moreover, the reduced imports were not replaced by working off crude inventories, as the right-hand column of the table shows.

TABLE 6 *Crude Oil Imports and Inventories, 1973–1974*

	Monthly average imports per district (millions of barrels)	Crude oil inventories at beginning of period (% of previous period)
September 1973 to October 1973	27.1	—
November 1973 to December 1973	23.7	99
January 1974 to March 1974	17.4	98
April 1974 to June 1974	27.8	101

SOURCE: Bureau of Mines, *Mineral Industry Surveys*. The import figures are averaged over P.A.D. Districts I, II, III, and V; the "previous period" is the preceding period of the same length.

it might cost the economy one million barrels of imports per day to impose the allocation regulations. If the difference between the first- and second-quarter import levels is attributed to the allocation program, then the Simon prediction was on the mark by the month of March.[12]

The third critical element in the crisis policy consisted of petroleum products allocation regulations.[13] The allocation program was set up to see that consumers received the "right" amounts of heating oil, diesel fuel, and gasoline. A number of schemes to distribute refined products were proposed in 1973, including full-scale World War II–type rationing with fuel stamps. The FEO decided to utilize a mixed program including price ceilings, domestic inventory controls, but last of all rationing.

"Take it by steps" was the program approach. If the embargo was fully effective, and inventory depletion was not able to satisfy demands,[14] the FEO would require refiners to produce a particular mix of products and to distribute that production in specified allotments to wholesalers and retailers.

Early in 1974 it was not yet clear that the embargo would be all that effective. Even so, the FEO put a limited set of allocation rules into effect, requiring a cutback in the production of gasoline and an expansion in the production of fuel oil. This was to provide security against a fuel oil outage during the late winter, but presumably not at the cost of a substantial gasoline shortage in the

12. It might be objected that the interrefinery allocation program was not the only cause for curtailment of imports—the embargo itself began to work at that time. But given a four- to six-week lag from curtailment in the Persian Gulf to reduced imports in the United States, this would imply that the embargo took effect in the Middle East in December, which is two months after the announced beginning. But there were no obvious changes of OPEC policies or controls in December to make it work then and not sooner.

13. Without retail ceilings on prices, the reduced supplies from the first two would merely have resulted in retail price increases to levels that cleared the lines at gas stations. Instead there were relatively constant prices and shortages. This can be blamed in part on the retail products.

14. Mandatory conservation would not have worked either. Reducing speed limits and Sunday gasoline sales would have cut consumption by only 0.4 million barrels per day, according to FEO estimates.

spring and summer. Imports were expected to decrease substantially, according to Department of Interior transmittals to the Federal Energy Office in November. But given substantial gasoline stocks, consumption cutbacks could be postponed until later in the year, when the embargo might be over or at least less severe.

Even this was an extremely pessimistic view. The half-dozen prominent forecasts available in October and November showed that the embargo was only partially effective, that total United States demand was decreasing, and that domestic inventories would replace part of any import reduction. The October forecasts in fact centered on supply reduction of only 1.8 million barrels per day with a range downward to a shortage of 3.0 million barrels per day.

As time passed these forecasts converged on a shortfall of 1.5 million barrels of available supply. By the middle of December it had become known to most analysts that the October estimates predicted too much reduction in imports. An Office of Management and Budget (OMB) study showed that "a slower economy, price increases, and conservation have reduced the estimated first quarter of 1974 shortage." Furthermore, the OMB proposed that some reduction of inventories in the hands of industrial and household consumers would eliminate any supply shortfall to less than a million barrels per day.[15] The Federal Energy Administration's *Petroleum Situation Report* indicated early in December that imports had failed to decline as much as was forecast, and demand had been reduced below that forecast. Each of these factors accounted for approximately half of the forecast adjustment—that is, half of the difference between the full embargo of 2.8 million barrels per day and the current prediction of 1.4 million barrels per day. The smaller shortfall implied a different set of policies than those invoked by the FEO. Rather than price controls, price increases on gasoline and fuel oil would have resulted in increased conservation sufficient to compensate for such a small

15. To the contrary the Conference Board showed at the same time that the first-quarter 1974 shortfall would be only slightly more than two million barrels per day.

supply reduction. In addition, inventory depletion could have made up for more than half the loss in imports.

The FEO chose more stringent policies because they used the more pessimistic forecasts. In January 1974 the Office of Energy Analysis reported a forecast domestic supply-demand "gap" of 2 million barrels per day in the first quarter and 2.5 million barrels per day in the second. But by the fourth quarter of 1974 there would be excess demands of 2.8 million barrels per day, with products inventories at such low levels that no more could be withdrawn. With such shortfalls, the expedient of reducing inventories was expected to delay the major impact of shortages, but the lack of inventories would then compound the problems appearing in the subsequent winter (fourth quarter, 1974). This view implied a mandatory shift of crude to fuel oil production at the expense of gasoline, as was put into effect in January 1974.

But this produced the predicted shortages. Early in 1975 motorists in many parts of the country began to experience significant gasoline shortages. The lines at stations formed after the required reductions in refinery output of gasoline and mandatory holdings of inventories together reduced deliveries to retailers. The retailers sold the restricted amounts of gasoline at controlled prices on a "first-come, first-served" basis.[16]

During the first quarter of 1974 the controls on old oil prices probably reduced supplies from domestic sources by 0.25 to 0.33 million barrels per day, and the interrefinery crude allocation scheme probably reduced imports by up to 1 million barrels per day. Shifting refinery outputs toward heating oil and away from

16. The choice of the pessimistic forecast can be defended. One reason was to reduce the chance of a catastrophic fuel oil outage if the import curtailment were worse than expected. But any policy designed to alleviate a potential supply-demand gap should have been flexible enough to deal with the occurrence of either no excess demand or severe excess demand. The FEO scheme was designed to be inaugurated under conditions of certainty and to remain unchanged for significant periods of time, refiners were to produce more fuel oil, and inventories were to be held off the market for the winter of 1974, no matter what actually happened to imports and domestic crude production. Thus the problem might not have been the choice of forecast but the built-in rigidity in these regulations.

gasoline reduced supply of gasoline by 0.8 million barrels. Given the forecasts that the supply-demand gap under a full embargo was going to be more than 2 million barrels per day, these actions made the forecasts roughly correct. The embargo itself was not effective, due to reduced demands from the downturn of the economy and warm weather, and to reduction of inventories. Regulation created the effects of the embargo, however, and the FEO gets the credit for the energy crisis perceived by consumers in 1974.

The gasoline shortages of 1979 were more of the same. With the withdrawal of Iran from world crude markets early in 1979, supply stringency was reduced by spot crude market price increases in world markets. Most consuming countries responded by reducing inventories, increasing wholesale and retail prices for gasoline and fuel oil, and bidding in the spot market for replacement volumes for the reduced Iranian supply. The United States did the opposite, by increasing inventories, holding down retail prices, and turning away from spot markets. The consequences included a reduced share of world trade in crude oil and domestic shortages of gasoline that year.

This sequence of events bears some relationship to that in response to the earlier embargo. Rather than allowing the market to adjust to less available crude, energy policy tolerated and eventually added to shortages. Supply reductions began in late 1978, when Iranian output fell from almost 6 million to less than 0.5 million barrels per day. Production in other countries increased, however, so that the net reduction of world supply in the first quarter of 1979 over the same period of 1978 was only approximately 2 million barrels per day. These conditions resulted in little change in domestic United States markets in the first quarter of 1979, but in the second quarter imports were down slightly.[17]

In contrast to crude markets, retail markets' supplies of gasoline were down more than half a million barrels per day in the

17. P. K. Verleger, "The U.S. Petroleum Crisis of 1979," *Brookings Papers on Economic Activity*, 2 (1979): 463–64, 469–70. Oil imports decreased slightly in 1979. (See table in footnote continuation, p. 64.)

second quarter. This reduction at retail was accomplished by having taken a number of small steps. Imports were in keeping with contract commitments, except for the reductions in Iranian supplies. There were attempts to replace these Iranian shortfalls with volumes available in the Rotterdam and other spot markets, but these were constrained by Department of Energy official and widely publicized statements seeking to discourage United States refiners from bidding up spot prices abroad.[18] The second small step was a reduction in domestic production, in keeping with systematic decline of capacity within the continental United States and also as a consequence of a leveling-off of previously increasing supplies from Alaska.[19] But the more important third step consisted of increases in second-quarter inventories in place of sales of gasoline. Production from refineries was approximately the same that quarter as in the same quarter the previous year, but inventories increased as a matter of policy by reducing deliveries to retailers.

Period		Imports (million barrels per day)
1978	1st quarter	8.33
	2nd quarter	7.79
	3rd quarter	8.53
	4th quarter	8.80
1979	1st quarter	8.73
	2nd quarter	8.01
	3rd quarter	7.57

SOURCE: DOE/EIA, *Monthly Energy Review*, January 1980, p. 16.

18. R. B. Mancke, "The American Response: 'On the Job Training'?" *Orbis*, Winter 1980, p. 791.

19. Quarterly averages of domestic petroleum production:

Period		Domestic production (million barrels per day)
1978	1st quarter	8.50
	2nd quarter	8.80
	3rd quarter	8.80
	4th quarter	8.70
1979	1st quarter	8.53
	2nd quarter	8.50
	3rd quarter	8.53

SOURCE: DOE/EIA, *Monthly Energy Review*, January 1980, p. 30.

At the same time aggregate demand continued to grow over the previous year, so that the demand for gasoline probably increased by 0.3 million barrels per day. Thus supply reductions of 0.5 and demand increases of 0.3 summed to 0.8 million barrels per day from early May to the end of July of 1979.

Price increases were rapid and extensive during that period, bringing the level of gasoline prices up to $.80 or $.90 per gallon from the previous-quarter level of $.50 per gallon. These increases were probably sufficient to reduce but not eliminate excess demand.[20] Department of Energy regulations prevented further price increases[21] and motivated the large increases in inventories. Both were required. In their absence, and with some further inventory depletion, there would have been sufficient supply to satisfy the increased demands at DOE ceiling prices and thus there would have been no shortages whatsoever.

The problem was that the DOE became concerned with the possibility of stock outage, and urged the refining and marketing companies to cut retail deliveries by 10–20 percent of those of the previous year. The DOE urged refiners to switch to fuel oil production earlier in the year so as to prevent fuel oil outages during the winter when Iranian curtailment would most likely reduce world market supplies further. This caused the building of stocks of both gasoline for the later summer and fuel oil for the winter.[22] Once again, as in 1974, the regulatory agency chose to cause a summer gasoline shortage to reduce the risk of empty fuel oil tanks in the winter. This would probably not have been the

20. Verleger, "The U.S. Petroleum Crisis of 1979," p. 469; H. S. Houthakker, P. K. Verleger, Jr., and D. P. Sheehan, "Dynamic Demand Analyses for Gasoline and Residential Electricity," *American Journal of Agricultural Economics*, May 1974, p. 415.

21. The price increases in 1979 actually exceeded those necessary to cover refiners' acquisition costs. Dealers' margins began increasing significantly in April 1979 and peaked in July—63 percent higher than in March (Verleger, "The U.S. Petroleum Crisis of 1979," pp. 467, 470).

22. Stocks of middle-distillate heating oil and diesel fuel were 15 percent lower in May 1979 than a year before. In response, DOE ordered that the stocks of middle distillates be built up—to a level exceeding the stocks for the same period in 1978 by nearly 9.5 percent (Mancke, "The American Response," p. 797).

market choice; and although the market makes mistakes, it had the luxury by use of higher prices of importing fuel oil to eliminate any winter fuel shortage.

Thus the gasoline crises of 1974 and 1979 were the products of decisions of regulators to hold inventories off the market. The results were shortages, extended beyond what could be tolerated on grounds that they were necessary for price stability. They were the product of attempts to play safe, and those attempts produced worse conditions.

Implementation of FEA Regulation During Normal Supply Periods

Operations under this regulatory system were vast in scale and scope. More than 300,000 firms were required to respond to controls, ranging from the three dozen major refining companies to a quarter of a million retailers of petroleum products.[23] The respondents had to file more than half a million reports each year, which probably took more than five million man-hours to prepare, at an estimated cost for reporting alone of $80 million. Most regulatory activity focused on the allocation regulations, since compliance with these regulations was determined from monthly reports from every refiner and marketer of heating oil, gasoline, and diesel fuel. But change itself added to the regulatory burden. As ownership of facilities changed, as new facilities were introduced, and as old plants shut down operations, new allocations were required. The regulatory process tracked not only recurrent transactions but every perturbation of supply and demand from month to month.

As inflation increased over the decade, increasingly complicated requirements were placed on producers, refiners, and marketers to account for cost increases to be allowed through as price

23. Cf. P. W. MacAvoy, ed., *Federal Energy Administration Regulation: Report of the Presidential Task Force,* Ford Administration Papers on Regulatory Reform (Washington, D.C.: American Enterprise Institute, 1977), p. 40.

increases. By 1976 regulatory operations forbade refiners either to pass through or "bank" for future justification of price increases the increased costs of construction and operation of additional refining capacity. Refiners were allowed to pass through increased depreciation and interest charges, but not stockholders' returns on additional capital. This was not a temporary lapse in the program, but a substantial disincentive to invest in the late 1970s given that costs of capital were rising sharply in the middle of the decade. And these restraints on capacity expansion were reinforced by the freeze on supplier-purchaser relationships, which prevented consumers from switching to new suppliers. In general the rules worked to prevent refiners from selling additional petroleum products at prices that failed to cover costs of increased refining capacity.

During the middle 1970s, in a sequence of case decisions, the FEA established the practice of issuing entitlements to the low-priced crude in the tier price systems so as to ensure availability of lower tier oil to all refiners. This began by giving any refiner with less than the national average ratio of domestic to imported crude in refinery runs an entitlement to purchase such crude at the lower controlled price from other refiners. Furthermore, small refiners with less than 175,000 barrels of crude refining capacity per day were given additional entitlements. This extra share was granted to small companies that together had approximately 20 percent of refining capacity. Because of this small-refiner bias, capacity expansion projects were smaller than optimal given the technology of the time, and plant utilization was excessive in small refineries already in operation. Since these were the least flexible and adaptable refineries, the industry was less able to alter the product mix as consumers demanded relatively more unleaded fuel in keeping with more stringent environmental requirements in the 1970s. During the middle 1970s the rate of growth of capacity of small and technologically simple refineries exceeded that of the rest of the industry by more than 100 percent.[24]

Thus the regulations had numerous and diverse effects. But most

24. Cf. ibid., Table 12, p. 68.

important were those from setting domestic crude oil prices at levels lower than world crude prices in the middle 1970s. This allowed domestic refiners with entitlements to the price-controlled oil to produce refined products at costs below those importing foreign refined products. The advantage was significant. Domestic crude oil prices for first-tier oil increased from 1976 to mid-1980 by $1.20 per barrel and second-tier prices increased by $2.40, but stripper and other uncontrolled prices increased by $24.00 per barrel. These disparities caused the costs of importers of refined products to increase from $4.00 to $9.00 per barrel, as shown by the excess of costs for imported over domestic price-controlled crude (see Table 7).

Mixing the regulated and unregulated crude supplies, the lower feedstock costs of domestic refiners theoretically could have been passed on to consumers as final product price reductions of $.10 to $.20 per gallon below those for all imported crude or refined products. But whether this occurred depended on other effects of controls on domestic supply.

One cancelling effect was that the deregulation policy begun in 1979 reduced base production levels for both lower and upper tier oil. These Carter administration provisions gradually decontrolled domestic crude, and among other items stipulated the following: (1) that the amount of oil allowed in the lower tier category would decrease 3 percent per month until total decontrol in 1981, and (2) that 4.6 percent of a property's upper tier output would be deemed "market-level new" oil and decontrolled on a monthly basis. Output from old fields constituted more than half the total in 1976, but only one-fifth the total in the first few months of 1980. As this new policy took effect, stripper production from old fields with unregulated prices actually increased in share of total crude oil output from domestic wells (as shown in Table 8). As expected, this increased domestic price levels, and the gap between domestic controlled and imported products prices narrowed.

The rapid depletion of lower tier sources also reflected reduced expenditures on maintenance of these reserves, in favor of extending stripper or newly discovered (price-unregulated) production.

TABLE 7 *Regulatory Price Differences Between Domestic and Imported Crude Oil, 1976–1980*
($ per barrel)

| Year | Refiner acquisition cost | | Difference |
	Domestic	Imported	
1976	8.89	13.48	4.64
1977	9.55	14.53	5.02
1978	10.61	14.57	3.96
1979	14.27	21.67	7.40
1980	24.23	33.89	9.66

SOURCE: DOE / EIA, *Monthly Energy Review*, various issues.

TABLE 8 *Domestic Crude Oil Quantities, 1976–1980*[a]

Year	Lower tier	Upper tier	Stripper	Alaskan North Slope	Naval reserve	Newly discovered and other unregulated
1976 (Feb.–Dec.)	54.4	31.5	14.1	—	—	—
1977	45.9	36.1	13.3	4.1	0.5	—
1978	37.5	34.4	14.0	13.0	1.1	—
1979	28.9	34.8	15.7	15.4	1.4	7.9
1980 (Jan.–Mar.)	20.5	29.6	15.5	16.0	1.5	16.7

[a] % of domestic sales at wellhead.

source: Joseph Kalt, *The Economics and Politics of Oil Price Regulation* (Cambridge, Mass.: Massachusetts Institute of Technology Press, 1981); from DOE / EIA, *Monthly Energy Review*.

This increased operating costs, and substituted higher for lower priced crude. In addition, the substantial increase in imported crude not only covered all increases in demands, but also replaced lower tier old domestic crude as that source became less available. These changes again reduced the gap between domestic controlled and imported product prices.

The extent of the enhancement of imports from the regulations is impressive. Indications are that it was necessary to increase imports to replace reduced domestic supply by close to 0.8 million barrels per day in 1976 and 1.1 million barrels in 1980 (as shown in Table 9). The switch to imported from domestic supplies by refiners substantially increased the cost of domestic crude runs, reducing any gains for consumers from crude price controls.

The "savings" in crude purchase-price reductions that might have accrued to consumers were also reduced by higher refinery operating costs inherent in the entitlement regulations favoring small and inflexible refineries. Other downstream cost increases due to inflation and changing market conditions were passed through in higher refining and marketing markups under the umbrella of the lower crude costs, given that the pass-through was no longer constrained by competition from imports and was furthered by regulatory requirements for uniform markups.

The entitlements system caused further erosion of the cost advantage. The small-refiner bias in disbursement of entitlements gave away part of the cost savings as a matter of course, since the imbalance in entitlements increased costs of those doing without them. With those doing without constituting the marginal sources of supply, final prices had to be higher to cover these costs.[25]

25. The cost disadvantage equals $V(b/e)$ where V equals the value of an entitlement, b is the percentage of total entitlements diverted by bias programs, and e is the percentage of total production not sharing in the bias program. In January 1978 the value of an entitlement was 6.2¢ per gallon, and 0.3¢ of that was diverted from those not receiving full shares. With the sharp rise in world prices after July 1979 the entitlement's value rose to 10.9¢, but cutbacks in bias programs kept the diversion to 0.3¢. Thus through most of the period those not receiving a proportionate share of entitlements had a cost disadvantage of one-third of a cent per gallon. If these unfortunate or politically inept refiners were the marginal sources of supply, then final prices would have to be higher by that amount.

TABLE 9 *United States Crude Oil Supply Under Various Conditions, 1976–1980*[a]

Year	Supply under market prices			Supply under controlled prices		
	Domestic	Imports	Total	Domestic	Imports	Total
1976	11.2	7.4	18.6	10.3	8.3	18.6
1977	11.5	7.4	18.9	10.7	8.1	18.9
1978	12.4	6.6	19.0	11.3	7.7	19.0
1979	12.1	7.2	19.3	11.4	7.8	19.3
1980	13.6	5.3	18.9	12.5	6.4	18.9

[a] Millions of barrels per day.

SOURCES: These estimates are simulations from a worldwide supply model as described in Paul W. MacAvoy, *Crude Oil Prices: As Determined by OPEC and Market Fundamentals* (Cambridge, Mass.: Ballinger, 1982): essentially a constant-elasticity supply-and-demand model with OPEC production stipulated at actual levels and with elasticities that simulate the 1960s and 1970s experience elsewhere. The model using actual average U.S. wellhead prices simulates supply and imports under regulation. The model using world prices for domestic supplies simulates the U.S. market without price controls. The stipulated elasticities of supply are 0.2 in the short run and 0.4 in the long run with a two-year adjustment period for the United States.

The sum total of these reductions in the "savings" was probably large enough to leave only $.03 to $.05 per gallon for the consumer through most of the middle and late 1970s. The domestic-foreign feedstock cost savings was probably $.06 to $.09 per gallon, of which $.03 went for increased refining and marketing costs and another $.02 went for overall regulatory costs (as shown by the "residual" in Table 10). This left $.02 to $.035 per gallon to be passed on to consumers, if not otherwise lost in the process. Only in 1980, after the doubling in foreign crude prices, was the amount left as much as $.10 per gallon.

As a result, little of the regulated crude price reduction actually reached consumers in the form of lower product prices. Indeed by 1977 it appeared that regulatory costs and entitlements had totally dissipated the regulatory cushion, causing domestic product prices to increase to world levels.[26] This may or may not have held later in the decade. One indication is whether domestic product prices were lower than imported products prices. Kalt found that the observed foreign-domestic refined products price differences increased, as a result of lower domestic prices, after the full-scale introduction of the domestic entitlements program. Also, Kalt found that changes in policies on entitlements caused changes in the difference between U.S. and foreign prices, particularly for gasoline and distillate fuel oils.[27] These differences, measures of

26. Cf. C. Phelps and R. Smith, *Petroleum Regulation—The False Dilemma of Decontrol,* Rand Corporation Report R-1951-RC, 1977.

27. Joseph Kalt, *The Economics and Politics of Oil Price Regulation* (Cambridge, Mass.: Massachusetts Institute of Technology Press, 1982), Chaps. 2 and 4. This work focuses on the relationship between U.S. and foreign gasoline, middle-distillate and residual fuel prices in order to examine the effects of EPAA/EPCA regulation. The data chosen by Kalt for comparison are the New York and Rotterdam spot market prices as reported by *Platt's Oil Price Handbook and Oilmanac.* A direct comparison reveals that the differences between the New York product price and the Rotterdam delivered price moved in a negative direction with the introduction of the entitlements program. New York prices of gasoline, middle distillates, and residual fuel were below the prices of foreign products starting in November 1974. The model for this simple difference in product prices would be

$$(P_{NY} - P_{ROT})_t = \beta_1 SUBSIDY_t + \mu_{t'}$$

TABLE 10 *Theoretical Maximum Reduction in the Price of Petroleum Products (¢ per gallon)*

	Total possible reduction	Increased costs of refining and marketing due to regulations	Cost of regulation in administration and operations	Residual
1974	7.9	3.2	1.5	3.2
1975	8.5	3.7	1.3	3.5
1976	6.2	1.5	2.2	2.5
1977	6.2	1.7	2.0	2.5
1978	5.0	1.5	2.5	2.0
1979	13.3	5.0	3.0	5.3
1980	25.9	11.8	3.7	10.4

SOURCE: Total possible reduction based on difference between the price of uncontrolled crude oil and the national average price of crude input to refineries, adjusted for refiner acquisition costs; DOE / EIA, *Monthly Energy Review*.

the gains to consumers, averaged close to $.05 per gallon. But this did not take account of higher retail margins in the United States, which could easily have dissipated a $.05 saving. By 1978 and 1979 retail markups were rising and being passed through in higher prices to final consumers, so that the "savings" went entirely in program leakage and regulatory cost increases.[28] Since this devolution was in good part induced by the regulatory process itself, gains to consumers in lower prices were both promised and then eliminated by regulation.[29]

---

where P_{NY} is the New York price per gallon; P_{ROT} is the Rotterdam price; *SUBSIDY*, the entitlements subsidy per gallon; $\mu_{t'}$ the stochastic component of $(P_{NY} - P_{ROT})$ due, for example, to random market disequilibrium; and β_1 is the marginal fraction of the subsidy passed through to domestic prices. Kalt provides an econometric investigation with adjustments and dummy variables in order to account for these different regulatory regimes. The econometric evidence supports the view that spot refined-product prices have been reduced by the entitlements program. But these spot market price differences do not reflect consumer purchase-price differences since they take no account of retail distribution margins. With rising retail margins in the United States the difference was probably cancelled before the final consumer purchase.

28. There is a quite different view of price behavior that merits careful consideration. In private correspondence, Paul L. Joskow contends that the entitlements / products price-control system was effective in passing a large fraction of the rents generated by price controls on to consumers. In support of his argument, Joskow cites changes in petroleum prices following decontrol in late January 1981. Wholesale and retail prices both rose sharply between January and March of that year.

The refiner acquisition cost of domestic crude increased $4.26 per barrel (10¢ per gallon), the acquisition cost of imported crude fell somewhat, and the average refiner acquisition cost increased by $2.62 (or 6¢ per gallon). During this same period of time retail prices of diesel fuel jumped 8¢ per gallon; heating oil, 11¢ per gallon; and gasoline, 12¢ per gallon.

The increase in product prices, Joskow argues, appears to be associated with the change in the prices of previously controlled domestic crude. This would not have happened if the product price controls were not binding. Releasing ineffective controls would have produced no market reaction.

29. That the lower wellhead prices were not passed on to consumers can be determined by a more formal analysis. The hypothesis is that wholesale prices in New York and Rotterdam would be the same, except for transportation costs, so that $P_{NY} = \alpha + \beta P_{ROT} + E$, with $\alpha =$ unit costs of transportation, $\beta = 1$, and $E = 0$. The exceptions would be during the OPEC embargo of 1974, and during the sharp reduction in Iranian supply in 1979, when the invocation of both price and allo-

Did petroleum control policy achieve its objectives of greater efficiency, reduced embargo vulnerability, and more equal income redistribution? Domestic crude production was replaced by imports, because of the depressing effect on domestic supply of first- and second-tier price controls. With imports enhanced as much as one million barrels per day, there must have been some increase in vulnerability to embargoes. The additional costs of resources to buy these imports could have been as much as $2–$3 billion per annum in the middle and late 1970s, so that efficiency losses were substantial. There was no compensating protection for consumers against adverse income effects and inflation from products price increases, beyond a few cents per gallon in the first two or three years of the program. By the end of the program, any such consumer gains had been dissipated in higher margins for refining, marketing, and retail distribution of gasoline

---

cation controls reduced U.S. prices. Then $P_{NY} = \alpha + \beta P_{ROT} + \gamma_1 D_1 + \gamma_2 D_2 + E$, with the hypotheses being that γ_1, $\gamma_2 < 0$ for dummy variables D_1, D_2 for these two time periods. Fitting these equations by least squares to data for gasoline and fuel oil, the results are as follows (with t-statistics shown in parentheses):

gasoline: $P_{NY} = 9.96 + .94 P_{ROT} - 41.97 D_1$
$(0.89) \quad (22.23) \quad (-2.79)$

$- 10.03 D_2 - 1.96 D_3; \quad R^2 = .95$
$(-0.54) \quad (0.20)$

fuel oil: $P_{NY} = 18.74 + .92 P_{ROT}^{(-2)} - 29.36 D_1$
$(2.05) \quad (12.48) \quad (-1.39)$

$- 84.27 D_2 + 4.07 D_3; \quad R^2 = .87$
$(-3.35) \quad (0.29)$

for 38 quarterly observations over the period 1972–1981 of prices measured in dollars per metric ton. The values of β are not significantly different from one, while those of the dummy variables differ from zero only for D_1 in the first equation and for D_2 in the second equation. Thus the hypotheses that Rotterdam and New York petroleum products prices are the same cannot be disproved. In addition, a dummy variable for control effectiveness between the two shortage periods (D_3) did not differ from zero, so that any price-depressing effects of controls had been quickly dissipated. (This does not take account of any further dissipation of the margin by higher margins at retail in the United States, since it accounts only for differences at wholesale.)

and fuel oils.[30] Because controls did not produce price reductions for final consumers, they failed to meet their goals of income redistribution. Thus none of the major intentions was realized, and indeed the results were counterproductive. In addition to their limited impact in achieving basic long-run policy goals, the allocation and price controls imposed additional short-run costs on the economy by exhausting gasoline shortages in both 1974 and 1979. In nearly every respect, policy initiatives in petroleum markets in the 1970s worsened market conditions.

---

30. If Joskow is correct in his view that regulation had an effect on domestic petroleum products prices, then two further economic consequences resulted from the price controls of the 1970s. First, consumers experienced the transfer of income in their favor, indicated by area C in the diagram. Second, given the regulated

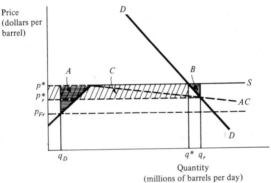

Quantity
(millions of barrels per day)

price, p_r, derived from rolling in or averaging the imported price, p^*, with the field price, p_{Fr}, there were deadweight losses in area B equal to the difference between costs to the economy of importing additional supply consequent from the price reduction, $(q_r - q^*)$. This loss is the difference between consumer demand for this additional output and the price that has to be paid to receive that output from foreign sources of supply. While area C is greater than area B (a rectangle of any width and length is always greater than a triangle of the same width and length), the value to society of that redistribution of income is not established by the amount of dollars involved so that the triangle may be "worth" more. Even if this is not the case, then both amounts may very well be negligible since the evidence used here at least roughly indicates that p^* and p_r are the same so that neither the consumer gain nor loss is of any appreciable magnitude.

3

◇—◇—◇—◇—◇

Natural Gas Policy

The natural gas legislation passed in 1978 was a massive undertaking, requiring the full attention that year of the energy subcommittees of the House and Senate, of a special House-Senate conference committee, and much of the time of the senior officials in the Office of the President concerned with energy matters. In part the Natural Gas Policy Act (NGPA)[1] required such an effort because it was the first building block in the Carter administration's energy plan. The NGPA also had to be done thoroughly and well because its potential effects on various consumer and producer groups were quite substantial. At that time gas supplies were short and any change in existing policy not only had to distribute benefits fairly, but to eliminate excess demand.

One difficulty in formulating the NGPA was that various groups saw only the set of results that affected them. Some saw only higher prices, while others saw more supply, from the new policy. Gas consumers with sufficient supply heard the call of *The New Republic* when that magazine stated: "[t]he great gas compromise consecrated with a fanfare on May 24th, may prove to be one of the lesser achievements of the 95th Congress. . . . . [I]t was not a compromise at all but rather a defeat for the buyers of natural gas . . . [and] a defeat for the federal government in that it set a date certain for the government to surrender its power to

1. 15 *U.S. Code, Annotated*, §§ 3301–3432 (Supp. 1979).

control the price of natural gas. In the future, if this compromise is enacted, that power will rest exclusively with the gas companies."[2] But for those experiencing shortage, *Harper's* was more to the point: "[G]overnment involvement in natural gas pricing has been a disaster. It is particularly discouraging to consider how much larger the natural gas market might have grown . . . if rigid price controls . . . had not been in place, resulting frequently in the shunning of new gas customers."[3] Both views were correct. Gas regulation had kept prices below equilibrium, causing shortages but also resulting in extraordinarily cheap supplies for other customers.

The NGPA was supposed to reduce shortages by means of a new regulatory process that would increase supplies and reduce demands. This process consisted of gradual price increases to add to exploration and eventual production, and also to dampen gradually the demands of final consumers.

The question is whether this legislation could possibly achieve so much. Congress and the regulatory agency carrying out the legislation could succeed, in the sense that by the end of the phasing period there would be no more shortage because additions to supplies and reductions in demands generated by the higher prices had cleared markets. On the other hand they could fail, given that shortages might well be as extensive at the end of the transition period as in the middle 1970s.

A second measure of success, however, is whether the price adjustments during the transition are "equitable." Without choosing the exact definition of "fair," it was clear that whatever was done had to maintain existing prices for consumers. But at the same time those benefited by the elimination of the shortage should pay the costs of additional supply, and those new benefiting from the shortage by buying at too-low prices should begin to pay the replacement costs of their gas supplies. The set of prices that would achieve all these goals with the smallest annual increments would qualify.

2. "A Lingering Death," *The New Republic*, June 10, 1978, p. 5.
3. Tom Bethell, "The Gas Price Fixers," *Harper's*, June 1979, p. 105.

Conditions in Gas Markets

During the 1960s and 1970s the federal government set prices for natural gas delivered into the systems of the interstate pipelines. The gas was produced from in-ground reserves under long-term contracts which allowed the purchaser to determine the rate of take during the peak heating season and high-demand years. The prices in these contracts were regulated by the Federal Power Commission (1954–1977) and the Federal Energy Regulatory Commission (1977 to date). Transportation was also regulated.

Interstate pipelines transport gas to retail distributing companies and industrial consumers to the north and west of the major producing fields in Texas, Oklahoma, and Louisiana. They have been subject to FPC and FERC controls of transportation rates and prices on their sales to retail gas utility companies in the major cities of the country, which in turn are price regulated by state public utility commissions. But gas has also been purchased for boiler use or space heating by industry located in or near the producing fields. These intrastate transactions were not regulated before the NGPA.

On the supply side, gas markets developed differently from other raw-material and fuel markets. Natural gas was first accumulated as a by-product in the search for oil in the years immediately following World War II, and was provided to the new pipelines at prices not much more than gathering costs. But when pipeline demands exceeded annual production rates from by-product reserves, prices began to rise and the consequent profits eventually led to exploration and expanded new reserve offerings. This supply-creation process consisted of undertaking exploration in prospect of finding additional gas-only reserves, and then committing any resulting additional "packages" of gas under new contracts at higher prices. These steps in fact resulted in aggregate additions to the supply of gas in the 1960s. With the supply process working as expected, production increased under new contract commitments to the interstate pipelines or to direct intrastate consumers.

The combination of slowly increasing supplies with rapidly increasing demands brought about large price increases in the 1950s. At that time prices on interstate contracts began to be regulated by the Federal Power Commission (FPC), based on a 1954 decision of the Supreme Court holding that the commission was responsible for wellhead contract prices as well as for delivery charges of the interstate pipelines.[4] During the 1960s the FPC maintained wellhead prices at approximately the level that was being realized in open markets just before regulation got under way. This was done through a regulatory process by which the commission developed "area rates" that kept new contract prices at the level of average historical costs of the reserves available in any region.[5] The system could not conceivably have worked to achieve price stability and sufficiency of supplies at the same time. Gas demand increases, partly as a result of lower prices for gas relative to other fuels, exceeded the GNP and total energy consumption growth rates each year. Commensurate supply increases were forthcoming only at marginal costs higher than average historical costs. In unregulated markets prices would have risen to the level of those higher marginal costs. But because controlled price ceilings were based on average costs less than marginal costs, the regulated prices could not bring about the necessary increases in supply.[6]

Shortages that inevitably followed this regulatory process were made larger by certain practices inherent in the gas regulatory

4. *Phillips Petroleum Co. v. Wisconsin,* 347 U.S. 672 (1954).

5. There were embellishments by which price ceilings were set somewhat higher on newly discovered reserves than on old contracts. But the higher tier new gas price ceilings were below current marginal costs, and the lower tier prices lagged behind even the historical costs of production from the reserves available.

6. A diagram can be used to illustrate this essential, if simplified regulatory effect. With annual demand of consumers served by the intrastate pipelines as reflected in DD, and field supply for these pipelines shown as SS, unregulated price would be p^* for production q^*. But the historical average costs of this supply would not be indicated by p^*, since SS is current marginal costs, but rather by AC. The average costs of supply sufficient to satisfy demand would be at level R. Setting regulated price at R, demand is q_D and supply q_S so that a shortage develops. (See figure in footnote continuation, p. 82.)

process. FPC controls did not extend to producer sales to intrastate buyers such as local power companies and industries. In the absence of controlled price ceilings, producers found the interstate market more attractive and units of growth of demands there, new and increasingly higher dedications were made there at prices higher than the regulated levels in intrastate markets. This market split between regulated and unregulated demands gave all the shortage to those interstate consumers supposed to be protected from higher prices.[7]

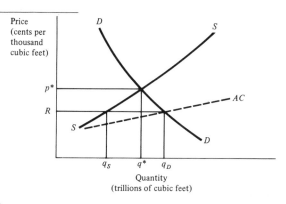

7. The accompanying figure depicts the special difficulty created by such regulation. There are two demand schedules for natural gas, one for intrastate sales and the other for interstate sales. The horizontal sum of the quantities demanded in each market at each price level gives the total demand for natural gas. Equilibrium is achieved where the supply curve intersects D, giving price p^* and quantity

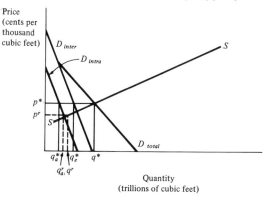

The system of regulation also made this situation worse by adopting certain quite rigid operating procedures. The accounting methods for finding costs to set rates were in fact not based on actual production costs, so that allowed current price changes lagged behind both current and historical exploration costs. This practice developed from the first rate decision in 1956 relating to sales in the Permian Basin of West Texas. The FPC staff and the gas producers used information on production costs for a then-current year in which regulation had already been in effect.[8] These costs which set current supply were determined by previously realized prices.

The process biased the results further by using quite general estimates of average costs, so that those considering development of the riskier deposits, with costs above average, were precluded from receiving returns sufficient to justify such an undertaking. In recognition of these higher costs at the margin, some attempt was made to add premiums to the high-tier ceiling prices. But the commission chose to specify the allowed premium on the low end of the range of actual costs, so that the disincentives from rate averaging were not substantially reduced.

The use of historical and average cost estimates to set prices had to create shortages. In fact a rapid decline in reserve additions set in during the late 1960s, and a serious shortfall of production to meet consumer demands in the North and East was realized during 1975–1978. Applying the process to set prices too low on only interstate sales gave this shortage to consumers of gas from only the interstate pipelines.

---

q^* which equals $(q_a^* + q_e^*)$ from intrastate and interstate markets respectively.

When price controls for interstate gas are set lower than p^*, gas producers will supply only q^r, since the cost of producing any additional unit exceeds that price. Intrastate buyers will actually increase consumption from q_a^* to q_a^r, while leaving only $(q^r - q_a^r)$ for interstate markets. Total quantity supplied is reduced from q^* to q^r, plus the intrastate share of the gas market increases, forcing the interstate market for natural gas to absorb the entire shortage.

8. Stephen Breyer and Paul W. MacAvoy, "The Natural Gas Shortage and the Regulation of Natural Gas Producers," *Harvard Law Review* 86 (1973): 941, reprinted in revised form in R. J. Kalter and W. A. Vogeley (eds.), *Energy Supply and Government Policy*, (Ithaca, N.Y.: Cornell University Press, 1976).

The Shortage of Natural Gas

Because of the peculiar institutions of the production contract, the shortage of natural gas in the 1960s was not recognized as a problem until long after it existed, in the middle 1970s. It began as a deficiency of reserves, as evidenced in an inability of the pipelines to contract for as much in new gas reserve "packages" as was demanded.[9] In the absence of enough new reserves, the pipelines in effect kept selling gas to new customers from previous accumulations of reserves committed to old customers. By the early 1970s, as final customer demands continued to increase, this previously committed reserve stock was insufficient to allow further expansion of production. The lack of additions to the stock in the early and middle 1960s finally constrained production growth. With consumer demand increasing further, shortages began to appear at seasonal peaks of demand in the upper Midwest and Atlantic seaboard regions.

Indications that this was going to occur could have been found in the reserve and production statistics (as in Table 11). Pipeline companies sought ten to twenty years of reserve backing for deliveries, to provide coverage for wholesale industrial buyers and retail gas companies. As they failed to obtain this backing, while still making new and expanded aid commitments for delivery, reserves stopped growing. By 1963 new reserves fell short of that sufficient to provide ten-year backing for new production. A point was reached by 1968 when that year's additions to reserves fell short of that year's production, so that reserve accumulations were negative that year. In eight of the nine succeeding years reserve levels similarly declined. By 1970 the interstate pipelines were short 45 trillion cubic feet of reserves to meet then-current demands at ten-year backing, and were short 107 trillion cubic feet at the more secure fifteen-year level of backing.[10] It had to be apparent that

9. Such demands for reserves were equal to additional final consumer demand for production, plus ten to twenty years of reserve backing for that production, for new and old final consumers at the price levels prevailing in the late 1960s.

10. Discoveries increased in 1970 due to large finds in Alaska so that total

the time would come when the pipelines would not be able to deliver as much as their buyers would call for that year.

That production shortage began to appear by the middle 1970s and was quite large by 1975. Forced curtailments of committed deliveries increased from 12 percent of total interstate demand in 1973 to 30 percent in 1975. Further curtailments caused the short deliveries to exceed 40 percent of the total in 1978 (as in Table 12).

In fact the shortage may have exceeded half of total consumer demands on the interstate pipelines. Purchasers put out of gas markets were in addition to those that were getting gas but with reduced deliverability. Regulatory rules against connecting new gas customers were put into effect in most northern metropolitan regions in the early 1970s. The excess demand of those excluded from gas markets was not listed as a "shortage," and yet substantial numbers of potential new residential and commercial customers denied service by state and federal regulations were "short" by the entire amount of their potential demands. Those industrial buyers making investment and production plans contingent on gas as the source of process raw material or fuel were "short" of supply when these plans had to be abandoned or shifted to petroleum products as the raw material. When these deficiencies are added to curtailments, then the total shortage was likely more than half of total demands.

This shortage condition was not evenly distributed across the industry and the country. The reduction of nationwide reserves by 86 trillion cubic feet from 1965 to 1978 included 98 trillion cubic feet of losses by the interstate pipelines and 12 trillion cubic feet of gains by intrastate consumers.[11] While national production increased by three trillion cubic feet per annum from 1965 to 1978, interstate deliveries rose by three trillion from 1965 to 1971, only

---

reserves were higher in 1970 than before or after; but this did not indicate new capability since these supplies were inaccessible to United States markets at the time.

11. Derived from Table 11 for national reserves, and as compiled from FPC Form 15 reports for interstate pipeline reserves alone.

TABLE 11 *Reserves and Production of Natural Gas (trillions of cubic feet)*[a]

| | Net additional reserves | Marketed production | Increase in production[b] | Net additional reserves required for additional production | |
				at 10-year backing[c]	at 15-year backing[d]
1955	11.9	9.4	n.a.	—	—
1956	14.0	10.1	0.7	7.0	10.5
1957	8.7	10.7	0.6	6.0	9.0
1958	7.5	11.0	0.3	3.0	4.5
1959	8.4	12.0	1.0	10.0	15.0
1960	1.2	12.8	0.8	8.0	12.0
1961	3.9	13.3	0.5	5.0	7.5
1962	6.0	13.9	0.6	6.0	9.0
1963	3.9	14.7	0.8	8.0	12.0
1964	5.1	15.5	0.8	8.0	12.0
1965	5.2	16.0	0.5	5.0	7.5
1966	2.9	17.2	1.2	12.0	18.0
1967	3.6	18.2	1.0	10.0	15.0

TABLE 11 (Continued)

1968	(5.6)	19.3	1.1	11.0	16.5
1969	(12.2)	20.7	1.4	14.0	21.0
1970	15.6	21.9	1.2	12.0	18.0
1971	(11.9)	22.5	0.6	6.0	9.0
1972	(12.7)	22.5	0.0	0.0	0.0
1973	(16.1)	22.6	0.1	1.0	1.5
1974	(12.8)	21.6	(1.0)	n.a.	n.a.
1975	(8.9)	20.1	(1.5)	n.a.	n.a.
1976	(12.2)	20.0	(0.1)	n.a.	n.a.
1977	(7.1)	—	—	n.a.	n.a.

[a]Estimates in parentheses are reductions; n.a.: not applicable.

[b]Difference between indicated year and preceding year.

[c]10 times increase in production.

[d]15 times increase in production.

SOURCE: American Gas Association, *Gas Facts*, 1977 Data (1978), p. 6 for net additional reserves, p. 23 for marketed production.

TABLE 12 *Forced Curtailments of Gas Deliveries by Interstate Pipelines (billions of cubic feet)*

| Year | Firm | Required cutbacks in deliveries | |
		Interruptible	% of total deliveries
1972	1031	285	9.5
1973	1362	218	12.0
1974	2418	276	21.9
1975	2976	444	29.5
1976	3400	449	35.3
1977	3197	416	36.9
1978	3150	433	41.7

SOURCE: Data for 1972–1973, Federal Power Commission, ad hoc special reports; for all other years, abstracts from Federal Regulatory Commission, Form 16 Reports of Gas Supply and Requirements.

to fall back to 1965 levels by 1978 (as shown in Table 13). The reason the interstate lines received all the shortage was that they were unable to bid against the intrastate purchasers to obtain more gas. Intrastate buyers were willing to pay 50 percent more by 1974, and 100 percent more by 1975, than regulated price levels (as shown in Table 14). The home-state utilities and industries were simply able to command priority by higher price bids, and thereby to give the shortage to regulated interstate consumers.

The Policy Problems

Both the size and the interstate share of the shortage became issues of increasing concern in federal energy policy by the middle 1970s. The first response was for the Federal Power Commission to increase area rates substantially. FPC Decision 770A adopted "forward-looking" and "comparative" cost-estimation techniques that justified increases in area rates on new contract gas in interstate commerce from $.50 to $1.42 per 1000 cubic feet (mcf). At the same time congressional "emergency" bills allowed industrial and commercial consumers in the North that were short of natural gas to go to Texas and buy in intrastate markets for shipment interstate at unregulated prices. This raised prices on sales to industrial consumers from two-thirds to parity with sales to retail consumers.

The interstate price adjustments in fact took off some of the excess-demand pressure. But FPC price increases were still insufficient to reduce, never mind eliminate, sustained interstate shortages. And attempts to respond further in this direction administratively were necessarily limited to allowing interstate buyers under curtailment to bid for a succession of short-term contracts in intrastate markets at competitive prices.

Limited regulatory reactions made it apparent that there would be continued and growing shortages for those protected by regulation. Since such constituencies were vanishing when low prices did not bring forth more service, Congress had to develop new

TABLE 13 *Gas Reserves and Production Dedicated to Interstate Pipeline Companies, 1965–1978*

Year	Year-end reserves[a]	Change from previous year[a]	Annual production[a]	Reserve / production ratio
1965	192.1	2.9	10.371	18.5
1966	195.1	2.9	11.137	17.5
1967	198.1	2.9	11.820	16.8
1968	195.0	(3.1)	12.552	15.5
1969	187.6	(7.4)	13.433	14.0
1970	173.6	(14.1)	14.092	12.3
1971	161.3	(12.2)	14.205	11.4
1972	146.9	(14.4)	14.207	10.3
1973	134.3	(12.6)	13.680	9.8
1974	120.5	(13.8)	12.965	9.3
1975	106.8	(13.7)	11.992	8.9
1976	98.3	(8.5)	11.389	8.6
1977	92.9	(5.4)	10.921	8.5
1978	94.0	(1.1)	10.865	8.7

[a]Trillions of cubic feet.

SOURCE: *Gas Supplies of Interstate Natural Gas Pipeline Companies*—1978, FPC Form 15, April 1980, Table 22, p. 65.

TABLE 14 *Average Acquisition Prices in Gas Pipeline Purchases, 1963–1979*

Year	Interstate price[a]	Intrastate price[a]
1963	35.7	49.7
1964	35.0	44.8
1965	34.5	42.2
1966	33.5	39.3
1967	33.0	39.6
1968	32.3	37.7
1969	31.3	38.3
1970	30.5	36.5
1971	30.8	36.5
1972	31.9	32.7
1973	32.9	39.5
1974	35.7	64.0
1975	42.1	96.3
1976	55.8	112.0
1977	76.5	131.2
1978	86.2	133.8
1979	114.9	142.4

[a] 1979 cents per million BTUs.

SOURCE: DOE / EIA, *Intrastate and Interstate Supply Markets Under the Natural Gas Policy Act*, October 1981, p. 40.

policy. Reducing the shortages required either regulating prices both in interstate and intrastate markets, or freeing the prices in interstate markets. The first option shifted the shortage so that all could share in it. The second, while reducing the shortage, involved higher purchase costs for established interstate residential consumers not yet subject to curtailments. In effect, no solution to excess demand problems could be found without a trade-off of more supply with an adverse price impact on consumers.

The Natural Gas Policy Act

The solution was in fact a merging of quite different House and Senate bills designed to deal with excess demands. The House sought to reduce the gas shortage by making regulation more comprehensive and binding. The Senate deregulated prices on the interstate wellhead contracts. This conflict was resolved in conference by eliminating controls on some classifications of gas but not on others and by extending the process of elimination of price controls over substantial periods of time. As the House-Senate Conference indicated: "Agreement reconciles two very different bills by redefining what qualifies as 'new natural gas.' The initial price for new natural gas is comparable to the one provided in the House passed bill, though it increases over time at a slower rate than the ceiling price for most of the gas that would have qualified as new natural gas under the Senate passed bill.[12]

The most elaborate plan for adjusting price levels was invoked for new gas prices, since that gas provided additional supplies for interstate markets: "Natural gas from new onshore production wells deeper than 5,000 feet is deregulated effective January 1, 1985, provided that such gas was not committed or dedicated to interstate commerce on April 20, 1977. Natural gas produced from new onshore production wells from a completion location shal-

12. *The Conference Report on Natural Gas,* Joint Explanatory Statement of the Committee on Conference, Senate Report 95–1126, 95th Cong., 2d sess. (1978), p. 68.

lower than 5,000 feet that was not dedicated to interstate commerce on April 20, 1977, is deregulated effective July 1, 1987, or as of the last date on which price controls are in effect if reimposed, whichever is later. Gas produced from new onshore production wells committed or dedicated to interstate commerce on April 20, 1977, is not deregulated."[13] The policy scheme was to deregulate the critical marginal supplies of gas at some future date, and to increase prices for these supplies at a rapid rate in the interim. Whether this would work would depend on whether the deregulated categories of gas were broad enough, and the allowed price increase generous enough, to result in substantially more supply in the middle 1980s. At the same time it was intended that the price increases at the wellhead be passed on to at least some final consumers. This was necessary to reduce demands specifically generated by too-low prices. But pass-through had to be more complicated than just that process designed to cut consumption, because home consumers had to be protected from large gas rate increases at the same time.

Pricing Provisions Under the NGPA

Although more than thirty classifications of natural gas in each of eight general categories were specified in NGPA, only three involved production eventually to sell at unregulated prices. The two quantitatively important categories were "new" and "high-cost" gas, which were price deregulated under four different classifications based on depth and location of the reservoir.[14]

These categories and price schedules limited the volume of potentially deregulated supplies. Their specifications in practice were quite exact: for example, new onshore production that qualified for "special development incentives" was subclassified according to whether the relevant wells were drilled to a depth less than or greater than 5000 feet; and although both shallow and

13. Ibid., p. 92.
14. 15 *U.S. Code, Annotated,* §3312 (Supp. 1979).

deep production wells were priced the same, each would have a future price schedule with a different time sequence (as shown in Table 15).[15] Price-decontrolled gas offshore was limited to that committed under contracts dated after April 20, 1977, but onshore new gas was decontrolled if it came from wells 2.5 miles beyond or 1000 feet deeper than existing "marker" wells.[16] Most production gas in 1978 did not fit these categories as a matter of course.

The time sequence of price increases as set was prolonged and unduly rigid. New gas prices were to increase from a level set at $1.75 per million BTUs on April 20, 1977, by 3.5 percent per year more than inflation until April 20, 1981, and by 4 percent per year more than inflation thereafter.[17] Other gas, including old offshore gas under new contracts and Alaskan gas, was to be priced at $1.45 plus inflation, but these supplies were to remain permanently under price controls.[18] Production from old renegotiated contracts was to comply with other regulated price schedules.[19] The difference between these schedules implies that Congress believed that "equitable" prices in the middle 1980s would be roughly 50 percent higher, but only for new gas.[20]

There was one further critical set of conditions centering on the rules in the NGPA for allocation of the higher prices to final consumers. Old gas supplies under contract to the interstate pipelines were assigned first to residential consumers, with any remaining volumes being allocated to commercial and industrial consumers. New gas was to go first to industrial consumers. The combination was to be repriced according to quite constraining schedules, but essentially residential consumers were to obtain gas at a price

15. Ibid., §3331. This is in contrast to old gas, consisting of reserves "dedicated to interstate commerce before November 9, 1978," which were not decontrolled and had price schedules that differed according to whether the gas was produced by small- or large-producer companies.

16. Ibid., §3312(c) (1) (B).

17. Ibid., §3312(b).

18. Ibid., §3319.

19. Ibid., §3316.

20. With both early and mid-1980s gas in 1978 dollars.

schedule equal to the "rolled-in" average of all outstanding field purchase prices[21] plus transportation average costs. Commercial and industrial consumers were to get supplies priced at the "incremental" field purchase price for new gas plus the transportation cost margin.[22] In practice this incremental price was to be constrained, however, by allocating to a "reserve pool" the difference between the price for new gas[23] and the BTU-equivalent fuel oil price. And any pool amounts would then be allocated among all consumers in the average or rolled-in price schedule.[24] Thus the alternative fuel oil price served as an effective ceiling on gas prices to be charged industrial customers.

This industrial gas price ceiling was supposed to vary by geographic region, since it was to be based on number two distillate fuel prices in some locations and residual fuel prices in other locations.[25] Such regulatory specifications made the choice of the comparable fuel oil price important for achieving gas deregulation. Using the higher number two price would tend to shift less of the gas field price increase to residential consumers and should lead to greater demand reductions by industrial customers. If set high enough, the incremental price ceiling would substantially reduce total demand and thereby cut back the shortage, perhaps even to the point where supplies were sufficient to meet remaining demands.

Given these new regulatory procedures, what policy outcomes could have been expected? One might be able to infer the intentions of Congress in enacting the NGPA in 1978 from what was predicted to result from the new legislation. Congress sought to engineer a "smooth transition" from regulation to decontrol if

---

21. 15 *U.S. Code, Annotated,* §§3341–43.

22. Ibid.

23. Also included were the higher prices for gas from new liquid natural gas (LNG) projects and from increased imports. The additional transportation costs for North Slope Alaskan gas, along with the higher prices from existing manufacture or synthetic natural gas (SNG) and currently approved LNG projects, would be "rolled in" or analyzed into existing price schedules for present consumers.

24. 15 *U.S. Code, Annotated,* §3344 (Supp. 1979).

25. Ibid., §3344(e).

TABLE 15 _Maximum Gas Price Ceilings Set by the Natural Gas Policy Act_

Section of the act	Price per million BTUs[a]	Category of gas	Date of deregulation
102	$1.75 + inflation[b] and escalation[c] ($2.34)[d]	_New natural gas_ —New Outer Continental Shelf (offshore) leases (on or after 4/20/77) —New onshore wells (1) 2.5 miles from the nearest marker well[e] (2) if closer than 2.5 miles to a marker well, 1000 feet deeper than the deepest completion location of each marker well within 2.5 miles —New onshore reservoirs	1/1/85
		Gas from reservoirs discovered on or after 7/27/76 on old (pre-4/20/77) Outer Continental Shelf leases	Not deregulated
103	$1.75 + inflation ($2.14)[d]	_New onshore production wells_ (wells the surface drilling of which began after 2/19/77, that are within 2.5 miles of a marker well and not 1000 feet deeper than the deepest completion location in each marker well within 2.5 miles)	
		—Gas produced above 5000-foot depth	7/1/87
		—Gas produced from below 5000-foot depth	1/1/85

Table 15 (Continued)

	Gas dedicated to interstate commerce before the date of enactment (rates previously set by FPC)	Not deregulated
104		
	—From wells commenced from 1/1/75 to 2/18/77	
$1.45 + inflation ($1.77)[a]		
	—From wells commenced from 1/1/73 to 12/31/74	
$ .94 + inflation ($1.15)[a]		
	—From wells commenced prior to 1/1/73	
$ .295 + inflation ($.36)[a]		
Applicable FERC rate + inflation	—Other gas (gas produced by small producers, gas qualifying for special relief rates, etc.)	
105	Gas sold under existing intrastate contracts	—1/1/85—if contract price exceeds $1.00 by 12/31/84
Contract price[f]		
	—If contract price on 11/9/78 is less than Section 102 price it may escalate, as called for by contract, up to Section 102 price	
	—If contract price on 11/9/78 exceeds Section 102 price then contract price plus annual inflation factor or Section 102 price plus escalation applies, whichever is higher	—If lower, not deregulated

TABLE 15 *Maximum Gas Price Ceilings Set by the Natural Gas Policy Act (Continued)*

Section of the act	Price per million BTUs[a]	Category of gas	Date of deregulation
106		*Sales of gas made under "rollover" contracts (an expired contract which has been renegotiated)*	
	The higher of $.54 or other applicable FERC price + inflation ($.65)[a]	—Interstate	Not deregulated
	The higher of expired contract price or $1.00 + inflation ($1.22)[a]	—Intrastate	1/1/85 if more than $1.00
107		*High-cost natural gas*	
	Deregulated	—Production from below 15,000 feet from wells drilled after 2/19/77	11/1/79
		—Gas produced from geopressurized brine, coal seams, Devonian shale	
	Applicable rate under the act or higher incentive rate as set by FERC	—Gas produced under other conditions the FERC determines to present "extraordinary risks or costs"	Not deregulated

TABLE 15 (Continued)

108	$2.09 + inflation (after 5/78) + escalation[c] ($2.50)[d]	Stripper well natural gas (natural gas not produced in association with crude oil, which is produced at an average rate less than or equal to 60,000 cubic feet per day over a 90-day period)	Not deregulated
109	$1.45, or other "just and reasonable" rate set by FERC, +inflation ($1.77)[d]	Other categories of natural gas —Any natural gas not covered under any other section of the bill —Natural gas produced from the Prudhoe Bay area of Alaska	Not deregulated

[a] Under the NGPA, if natural gas qualifies under more than one price category, the seller may be permitted to collect the higher price.

[b] These prices include an "annual inflation adjustment factor" in order to adjust prices for inflation. The price for a given month is arrived at by multiplying the price for the previous month by the monthly equivalent of the annual inflation factor. Since most of the prices set by the NGPA are as of April 20, 1977, the adjustment for inflation begins in May 1977.

[c] These prices will escalate monthly, in addition to the inflation factor, by an annual rate of 3.5% until April 1981, after which they will escalate by 4%.

[d] The estimated maximum ceiling price as of December 1979, rounded to the nearest cent, due to operation of inflation and escalation adjusters.

[e] A marker well is any well from which natural gas was produced in commercial quantities after January 1, 1970, and before April 20, 1977, with the exception of wells the surface drilling of which began after February 19, 1977.

[f] The average price reported to the FERC for intrastate gas sales contracted for during the second quarter of 1978 (just prior to the enactment of the NGPA) was approximately $1.90.

SOURCE: Federal Energy Regulatory Commission, *Annual Report, 1979* (Washington, D.C., 1979), Appendix pp. 65–66.

the price ceilings were predictively high enough to mitigate market imbalances.

The assertion that shortages would be eliminated by 1985 could not have been supported at the time of passage of the NGPA, however. Forecasts at that time did not indicate that NGPA-decontrolled prices would reach levels necessary to approximate open-market prices in the middle 1980s and permit the "smooth transition" to decontrol.

The basis for expecting any such results would have been the predictions of experts in 1978. At that point in time the Department of Energy large-scale econometric model produced a widely used forecast of supply-and-demand conditions in gas markets in the early 1980s (as in Table 16). The DOE forecast that if the NGPA-prescribed price series were followed, and if economy-wide inflation were approximtely 5 percent per annum, the average United States residential gas price would increase about 6 percent per year in current dollars between 1978 and 1985. The price of gas to commercial and industrial buyers, assuming incremental pricing constrained by the "pool," would rise by almost 9 percent per year even with the cutoff of gas price increases at residual oil price levels.[26] With such NGPA prices, industrial demand would be decreased by one-third and production supply would be increased by one-fifth, so that the shortage would be reduced by only one half that expected under continued regulation without the NGPA.

Of course this was not the only prediction available to Congress in 1978. At the other end of the political spectrum the industry trade association (the American Gas Association) used its TERA econometric model to predict that excess demands under continued regulation would increase by 20 percent if there were no curtailment program.[27] The AGA gas forecasts included both

26. DOE, *Energy Supply and Demand in the Mid-Term: 1985, 1990, and 1995* (1979); DOE, *An Evaluation of Natural Gas Pricing Proposals* (1978).

27. American Gas Association, *Offshore Gas and Oil Supply Model* (Arlington, Va., 1977); American Gas Association, *Onshore Gas and Oil Supply Model* (Arlington, Va., 1978); American Gas Association, *Demand Market Place Model* (Arlington, Va., 1979) (vols. 1–3, respectively, of Total Energy Resource Analysis (TERA) Model documentation).

TABLE 16 *1978–1979 Forecast Effects from the Natural Gas Policy Act (trillion cubic feet)*

Market condition	1985 forecast level without NGPA	Changes in 1985 due to NGPA	
		At low oil price[b]	At high oil price[c]
Supply			
Conventional source	16.7	+0.6%	+0.6%
Supplemental sources	2.6	+4.4%	+4.9%
Total	19.3		
Demand			
Residential and commercial	7.9	+0.6%	+3.1%
Industral	9.8	−3.4%	+1.1%
Other[a]	2.5	+6.0%	+7.0%
Total	20.2		

[a]Includes raw material, refinery, electric utility, and pipeline fuel use of natural gas.

[b]DOE Simulation Series ''C-Low''—medium supply, medium demand, world oil at $15.00 per barrel.

[c]DOE Simulation Series ''C-High''—medium supply, medium demand, world oil at $21.50 per barrel.

SOURCES: DOE, *Energy Supply and Demand in the Mid-Term: 1985, 1990, 1995* (1979); DOE, *An Evaluation of Natural Gas Pricing Proposals* (1978).

conventional and supplemental supply, and showed that under the NGPA the volume available from conventional sources would actually be reduced by 2 percent. The AGA expected that conventional gas supply under the NGPA would fall short of demand, because petroleum prices of less than $5.00 / mcf would set a cap on gas supply prices too low to allow the critical supplemental supplies to clear out industrial demands for gas. Supplies from Canada and Mexico would be available, however, to expand the total by 10 percent, and synthetic gas from coal would contribute 19 percent more, for a total increase of 24 percent. This would more than meet additional demands, at prices of roughly $5.00/ mcf for Canadian and Mexican gas, and of $5.70–$6.50 for synthetic gas, most of which would be higher than BTU-equivalent petroleum products prices.

Thus both government and industry experts predicted that as a consequence of the NGPA there would be excess gas demands. It was reasonable to have expected the NGPA to work to squeeze excess gas demands into other markets, but not to eliminate them. The NGPA was not intended to deregulate, given that it was not going to bring regulated prices to open-market levels by 1985. The continued NGPA squeeze was to be on industrial gas demands. Most of the growth in residential and consumer demands was to be met by NGPA allocations of additional supplies to these sectors. Gas in an open market destined for industrial consumers was to be reallocated to home consumers, and with only very small total supply increases there would have to be continued shortages of industrial gas. As a matter of course this shortage would never be seen on gas wholesale and retail markets, because potential industrial consumers would invest in equipment to burn alternative fuels and permanently leave gas markets after failing to obtain supplies.

Short-term Economic Effects of the NGPA

During the first four years of operations under the Natural Gas Policy Act gas market performance improved significantly. The industrywide shortages of 1975–1978 were reduced to low levels and to shortfalls for consumers only in certain specific heating markets. There have been only insubstantial curtailments since 1980. In fact pipeline companies, in conjunction with retail gas utilities, have added new customers to delivery systems.[28] The market has been transformed from a classic disequilibrium of excess demand to that of supply-demand balance.

Five economic explanations can be given for this remarkable change from market disequilibrium to full balance of supply with demand. First, new gas supplies have increased to a greater extent than anticipated in NGPA-related forecasts. Prices of natural gas in unregulated intrastate markets increased rapidly following the 1973–1974 OPEC price increase, and the interstate regulated prices also increased after the rate increase decisions of the FPC in 1974 and 1976.[29] As a consequence exploration and development drilling increased, with footage drilled more than doubling from 1970 to 1979. More gas was discovered and brought to market than had been expected under continuance of the old regulation.

Under the Natural Gas Policy Act substantial price incentives were provided to suppliers of new reserves obtained through the discovery process. In the year after the enactment of the NGPA new discoveries of natural gas reserves increased significantly. The volume of total new discoveries, revisions, and extensions increased 35 percent between 1978 and 1979.[30] Drilling for new gas expanded, and the total number of wells completed under sections 102, 103, 107, and 108 of the NGPA was 54 percent higher

28. American Gas Association, *Gas Facts—1980* (a statistical survey of the gas utility industry), (Arlington, Va., 1980), p. 73.

29. Opinion and Order Prescribing Uniform National Rate for Sales of Natural Gas Dedicated to Interstate Commerce on or After January 1, 1973, for the Period January 1, 1975, to December 31, 1976, 10 Federal Power Service 5–293 (July 27, 1976) (Federal Power Commission Opinion Number 770). The reader can find a history of the 1974 decision in this opinion.

30. American Gas Association, American Petroleum Institute, and Canadian Petroleum Association, reserves of crude oil, natural gas liquids, and natural gas in the United States and Canada as of December 31, 1979, as shown in *Gas Facts—1980*, "Estimates of Proved Reserves of Natural Gas in the United States, 1955–1979," p. 6.

in 1979 than in 1978.[31] But whether the additions are substantially greater than what would have been achieved with the continuation of regulation under the previous Natural Gas Act remains to be determined. Moreover, much of the Section 103 category gas from new discoveries replaces production that would have come from old reserves found in sections 104–106 categories. Even so, supplies of gas that otherwise would not have been forthcoming without the pricing schedule of the NGPA probably have since been discovered, developed, and are in the process of production. Increased supply from operations under the Natural Gas Policy Act has had some effect in reducing the deliverability shortage experienced in 1976–1978.

Second, mandatory uniform pricing of intrastate and interstate gas under the NGPA put the interstate pipelines back into the purchase market for additional gas reserves and production. These pipelines gained access to the more abundant intrastate gas which they used to expand service to residential and other buyers not on the system in the mid-1970s.

As a result of these two changes, a "gas bubble" of additional supply in excess of immediate demands developed for the interstate pipelines. The size of the "bubble" in the 1979–1980 heating season was probably in the range of 2–3 trillion cubic feet. During that winter at least 0.5 trillion cubic feet of this deliverability was sold to Pacific Lighting, United Gas, Transcontinental Gas Pipeline, Northern Natural Gas Pipeline, and Texas Eastern Transmission Company, and lesser amounts to Natural Gas Pipeline and others. These volumes were mostly provided by the intrastate Oklahoma pipelines and Texas oil and gas companies.

Another important factor in the elimination of general shortages was the substantial slowdown in the rate of economic growth throughout the economy, which reduced the growth of natural gas demand not only in the industrial but also the commercial and residential sectors. Natural gas demands were also directly affected

31. "The Current State of the Natural Gas Market; An Analysis of the Natural Gas Market and Several Alternatives, Part 1," DOE / EIA–0313, December 1981, p. 22.

by the higher gas prices consequent upon the higher field prices encountered in the early and middle 1970s. By 1980 substantial conservation impacts were being registered in gas markets for the first time.[32] These income and price effects leveled total consumption demands in the early 1980s.

The fifth factor has been the operation of the Fuel Use Act of 1979 and the Energy Supply Act of 1975 to curtail industrial gas demands as a matter of public policy. The effectiveness of these pieces of legislation is difficult to assess because they require only in general terms that powerplants should not schedule operations based on natural gas, leaving it unclear as to whether new powerplants built on coal boilers would indeed have used gas given the option. There has been some fuel switching out of gas and oil to coal because plants have been converted (as shown in Table 43). As oil and gas prices have increased, those plants most adaptable to switching from gas to coal changed over their operations within a fairly short period. As old plants gradually were transformed to standby power operations, new capacity dedicated to coal and nuclear fuel utilization further reduced the industrial demands for gas. Although not exactly determinable at this time, industrial, and thus total, demands for gas were probably reduced by legislation that was part of President Carter's energy policy.

These factors explain the elimination of market disequilibrium at the end of the 1970s.[33] The NGPA integrated the intrastate and

32. *Gas Facts—1980,* Table 52, "Annual Consumption of Energy Resources by Major Sources in the United States by Consuming Sectors, 1973–1980," p. 64, shows that 1980 experienced a decline in each consuming sector for almost every source of energy. This is the first overall decline since 1974. This general reduction in use can be explained by a combination of effects and the downturn of the economy that year.

33. To indicate how they worked together, the following diagram illustrates the steps in the process. Regulation of only interstate sales before 1978 produced one set of results, while that under the NGPA after 1978 of both interstate and intrastate sales produced quite different results. Before 1978, with interstate price set at regulated level R, all additional supplies along supply curve S' were going to intrastate purchasers with demands D_2. The intrastate market cleared at unregulated price P_2 for quantity Q_2. But interstate purchasers along demand curve D_1 seeking quantity Q_1 at the regulated price R obtained only Q_1'. Thus $Q_1 - Q_1'$

interstate markets for natural gas, setting a regulated price sufficient to clear the market of excess demand and canceling out the
shortage. However, the NGPA specified a rigid schedule of prices
that will hinder adjustment to new market conditions over time.
Thus it cannot be expected that equilibrium will be maintained
indefinitely.

---

constituted the interstate shortage. But after 1978 under the NGPA the additional
supplies S' were available to both intrastate and interstate purchasers at a new
higher regulated price R^* sufficient to clear the market of excess demands. This
new regulated price brought forth some additional supplies; but given essentially
stagnant demand in recent years, existing supplies were sufficient when in part
reallocated to interstate buyers to dissipate their gas shortages of the middle 1970s.

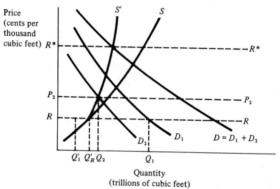

Regulated Interstate Price R and Unregulated Intrastate Price P

The diagram shows purchase demand functions for interstate and intrastate
pipelines. D_2 is intrastate demand, D_1 is interstate demand, and total demand is
$D = D_1 + D_2$. The price R is the average regulated ceiling price at the wellhead set
before passage of the NGPA, and the price R^* is the regulated price after the
NGPA was enacted. Prior to the NGPA the intrastate market was not regulated,
so that additional supply cleared that market at P_2 for quantity Q_2. But at the
regulated price, demand in the interstate market, Q_1, exceeded its share of the
total regulated supply, Q_1'. After the NGPA the regulated price of gas, R^*, was
sufficient to clear total demand, D_1, and the additional available supply, S'. Because
of lags in development of new supplies, and because only supplies along the
intrastate supply curve S' were developed prior to the NGPA, the post-NGPA
supply curve is assumed to remain at S'.

Long-term Economic Prospects Under the NGPA

Several consequences of the NGPA price schedule threaten to move the market away from equilibrium, and increases in demand heighten the possibility of significant market disruption in the mid-1980s. Problems stemming from the act include differential costs of gas supplies faced by interstate and intrastate pipelines and resulting allocation effects, incentives for inefficient development of high-cost gas, and inefficiently low ceiling prices. Other complicating factors include conditions of increased demand and reduced supply availability likely to occur at the time of partial decontrol in 1985.

Although all pipelines face the same prices for unregulated or deregulated natural gas, their supplies do not consist of the same mix of unregulated (new and high-priced) and regulated (old and low-priced) gas. Because intrastate pipelines obtain about 80 percent of their supplies under unregulated prices, their average costs will be much higher than those of interstate pipelines, whose throughput consists of only 30 percent unregulated gas.[34] Interstate pipelines will have the lowest current average prices for wellhead production, so that they will be able to bid the highest prices for additional supplies. The resulting allocation of new reserves could be politically and economically unacceptable. Proportionally more supplies would be available to the New England and West North Central regions (through interstate pipelines), and proportionally less to the Southwest producing regions themselves (served by intrastate pipelines).[35] Pipelines low in "old" supplies

34. Milton Russell, "Natural Gas Deregulation: Overview of Policy Issues," *Resources for the Future*, April 1982, p. 21.

35. New production would be misallocated between pipelines in favor of those with large relative volumes of low-priced gas (their demands would be artificially increased by their reduced resale prices). But when the partial decontrol of gas prices occurs as required by the NGPA, the short-run price will rise from the rolled-in equilibrium price R along average purchase cost curve AC to the marginal supply price P_1 along supply curve S' (in the diagram). Since the supplies along supply curve S are not currently being developed, and because of lags in the development of gas production, gas will be supplied from curve S' in the short run. In the long run, real price will fall from P_1 to P^* as supplies of gas from

could realize shortages from an inability to purchase new supplies, and therefore an inability to offer services equally with those of other regions of the country.

Inefficiencies in exploration and development result from institutionalizing specific categories of old and new production. Development of "new" and "high-cost" sources of supply is encouraged, and the reworking or maintenance of old fields is discouraged. Because of these categories and their price differences, high-cost and new gas in effect displace supplies that would follow from maintaining established deliverability from old

---

reworking old fields and maintaining old wells become available, and as the actual supply curve moves from S' to S.

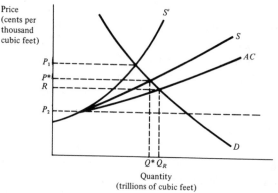

Price Spikes on Decontrol without Shortage Conditions

This diagram shows the supply of new deregulated gas, S', and the supply of additional new and old supplies, S, that would occur under uniform price conditions. The long-run effect of deregulation is to raise the price from the regulated price R to the market clearing price P^*, since supply moves to the more efficient curve S. The increase is not caused by excess demand as would appear from a one-time price spike. In the short run the additional supplies from reworking of old fields are unavailable, and the supply will come from curve S'. The lag problems for the development of these sources will cause the short-run price to rise from R to P_1, and eventually, when development catches up, the price will fall to P^*. Thus the price spike in 1985 is reflected in the diagram by an increase from R to P_1.

fields.[36] In fact the number of wells qualifying for deep-well status (a "high-cost" category, section 107) has increased markedly since 1977—from fewer than 50 in 1977 to approximately 350 in 1980. From 1979 to 1980 estimated production of high-cost gas doubled in response to prices averaging more than 2.5 times the national average gas price. Some high-cost gas is selling at prices over $8.00 per million BTUs.[37]

Finally, although price increases under the NGPA were initially substantial, the schedule of increases is based on crude oil priced

36. Such a phenomenon is described in the following diagram, where the producers are provided incentives to move along curve S' rather than S as a consequence of only "new" and "high-cost" supplies being offered prices in the range from P^* to P_2.

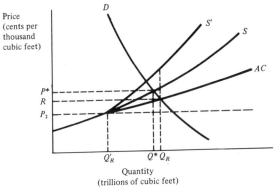

NGPA Price Categories and Resulting Supplies

In this diagram S' is the supply of new gas, primarily sections 102 and 107 deregulated supplies, and S is the total supply of gas. The greatest supply efficiency is obtained at price P^* and quantity Q^*, where demand is met with "new" supplies as well as supplies from reworking and pressure maintenance. R is the regulated price, equal to the average or rolled-in costs AC for market clearing quantity demanded Q_R. But supplies Q_R are generated from S', even though they are sold along curve AC. This is because supply produced along S' at higher prices is averaged with all other deregulated gas to produce the average cost curve. Q_R' is the quantity of old, price-regulated gas produced under regulation, and P_2 is the corresponding price for these supplies.

37. DOE/EIA, *Monthly Energy Review,* February 1981; DOE/EIA, *The Current State of the Natural Gas Market,* December 1981.

at $15.00 per barrel. This sizable lag behind competitive fuel prices has increased demands for gas relative to other fuels in the long run. Although these increases have not been evident to date because of the other demand-reducing factors already discussed, the effects will be realized over the next five years.

In addition to these three problems resulting from the NGPA's special provisions for old, new, and high-cost gas, conditions are present which are likely to bring about substantial reserve and deliverability shortages in the middle 1980s. As partial deregulation takes place under the NGPA in 1985 and 1986, this disequilibrium will cause a large "price spike" in deregulated and average contract prices. The causes of this potential disequilibrium include: (1) the lack of growth in production, as a direct consequence of the present low reserve/production ratios, and (2) the likelihood of substantial increases in demand through the period of recovery from the 1982 recession. The consequent shortage of reserves is necessarily translated into a "price spike" on new contract commitments.

At the present time reserve/production ratios are still at the fifteen-year low (see Table 17). Substantial volumes of "old" gas are to the point of depletion, where reworking of producing facilities is necessary. But with present high and rising costs of secondary recovery, many of these facilities will be reduced to stripper status rather than be engaged in secondary recovery in the next few years because the costs of reworking are too high given present regulated price levels. The early abandonment of wells wastes potential supply, to such an extent that it is not unreasonable to expect that total supplies will barely stay constant over the next few years.

Expected increases in demand will worsen these market conditions. The sharply higher world crude oil market prices caused demands for gas to increase to an extent unpredicted at the time the NGPA was passed. The doubling of crude prices in 1979–1980 took competitive fuel prices to levels much higher than allowed under the NGPA for comparable residential and industrial gas (as shown in Table 18). Home gas in early 1981 was priced

TABLE 17 Total Gas Proved Reserves Dedicated to Interstate Pipeline Companies, Changes in Gas Proved Reserves, Production, and Reserve/Production Ratios, 1965–1980

Year	Year-end reserves[a]	Change from previous year[a]	Annual production[a]	R/P ratio
1965	192.1	2.9	10.37	18.5
1966	195.1	3.1	11.14	17.5
1967	198.1	2.9	11.82	16.8
1968	195.0	(3.1)	12.55	15.5
1969	187.6	(7.4)	13.43	14.0
1970	173.6	(14.1)	14.09	12.3
1971	161.3	(12.2)	14.20	11.4
1972	146.9	(14.4)	14.21	10.3
1973	134.3	(12.6)	13.68	9.8
1974	120.5	(13.8)	12.96	9.3
1975	106.8	(13.7)	11.99	8.9
1976	98.3	(8.5)	11.39	8.6
1977	92.9	(5.4)	10.92	8.5
1978	94.0	(1.1)	10.86	8.7
1979	97.3	3.3	11.54	8.4
1980	97.1	(0.2)	11.60	8.4

[a]In trillions of cubic feet.

SOURCE: Gas Supplies of Interstate Natural Gas Pipeline Companies—1980, FPC Form Number 15, December 1981, Table 22, p. 78.

TABLE 18 *Gas and Heating Oil Prices*

	Gas price over heating oil price (%)	Gas price (current $/million BTUs)	Change from previous year (%)	Heating oil price (current $/million BTUs)	Change from previous year (%)
		To residential users			
Jan. 1977	64.9	2.076[a]	—	3.197[h]	—
Jan. 1978	67.2	2.346[b]	13.0	3.492[i]	9.2
Jan. 1979	73.6	2.844[b]	21.2	3.866[j]	10.7
Jan. 1980	52.7	3.446[c]	21.2	6.538[j]	69.1
Jan. 1981	48.0	3.950[c]	14.6	8.230[j]	25.9

TABLE 18 (Continued)

		To steam-electric utilities			
Jan. 1977	51.2	1.111^a	—	2.172^a	—
Jan. 1978	63.1	1.333^e	19.98	2.113^h	2.72
Jan. 1979	65.8	1.502^f	12.68	2.281^b	7.95
Jan. 1980	46.0	1.948^g	29.69	4.235^b	85.66
Jan. 1981	47.1	2.541^g	30.44	5.399^i	27.49

[a] DOE/EIA, *Monthly Energy Review*, August 1978, p. 81.
[b] DOE/EIA, *Monthly Energy Review*, August 1980, p. 84.
[c] DOE/EIA, *Monthly Energy Review*, April 1981, p. 88.
[d] DOE/EIA, *Monthly Energy Review*, August 1978, p. 84.
[e] DOE/EIA, *Monthly Energy Review*, August 1980, p. 85.
[f] DOE/EIA, *Monthly Energy Review*, April 1981, p. 89.
[g] As provided by telephone on May 29, 1981, by Mr. R. Solkov of DOE Federal Energy Regulatory Commission statistics section.
[h] DOE/EIA, *Monthly Energy Review*, August 1978, p. 72.
[i] DOE/EIA, *Monthly Energy Review*, August 1980, p. 81.
[j] DOE/EIA, *Monthly Energy Review*, April 1981, p. 77.

at half the level of heating fuel, and industrial boiler gas was also available at half the price of residual fuel oil. This gap between petroleum and gas products prices shifted demands to gas and away from oil at rates not forecast to occur under the NGPA.

In addition, substantial increases in demands from those presently on distribution systems are likely to occur. The tendency of pipelines and retail distributors to add final consumers has been carried to extensive lengths. Pipelines and distributors have competed heavily to get additional final consumers in the market for fuel oil, propane, and liquefied petroleum gas (LPG) suppliers—to a greater extent than is warranted by availability. These conditions of newly created demand will be realized in extremely high demand growth when the economy moves out of recession into full expansion, and gas consumers once again demand volumes in keeping with a high level of economic activity. The "gas bubble" will have long since disappeared.

With growth rates of 3–4 percent in real income and productive activity to be expected each year, residential, commercial, and industrial demands should increase 3–5 percent in each of the next three years (assuming that the short-run income elasticities of demand groups average roughly +0.3 each year, or in the long-run +0.7 during the 1982–1985 period).[38] Such rates of increase imply the volumetric levels of demand shown in Table 19.

Roughly stable supply and increasing demands produce excess demand under regulation. As price controls are partially eliminated as required by the NGPA in 1985 and 1986, the new contract prices for certain categories of supplies will increase to eliminate that excess demand. The extensive but still incomplete deregulation in those two years will focus the categorical increases on approximately half the volume of the total supplies. Fixed supply and increased demand are likely to produce price increases of

38. The short-run income elasticities used for the calculations in Table 19 are consistent with the long-run elasticity of 0.6 taken from the MacAvoy-Pindyck Natural Gas Econometric Model (P. W. MacAvoy and R. S. Pindyck, *The Economics of the Natural Gas Shortage* [*1960–1980*] [Amsterdam: North-Holland; New York: American Elsevier, 1975], p. 248). The short-run elasticities also conform to the postpublication MacAvoy-Pindyck Model.

39 percent in 1986 over 1984. This and later changes in price levels are shown in Table 20.

This price spike will be highest in intrastate markets where supplies will consist predominantly of deregulated gas. Having a smaller relative volume of "old" gas production, the intrastate pipelines and retail distributors will have the highest average prices for wellhead production and will experience the greatest increases. The regional disparity due to differential costs of supplies for intrastate and interstate pipelines will be exacerbated as additional supplies for commercial and industrial development in the Southwest will be cut off in order to subsidize residential and commercial consumption in the North.

Pipeline / producer contracts already indicate that prices may rise above the market clearing level. Indefinite price escalator clauses and "most favored nation" clauses have permitted high degrees of competition for future supplies in the face of declining additions to reserves. As a result, contract contingency clauses register price specifications for natural gas at well over the equivalent price for a competitive fuel.[39]

Thus present conditions are deceiving. It is now likely that the growth in demands generated by low gas and high oil prices will be fully realized just as price controls are supposed to be phased out on half the production in 1985. Even though there is excess deliverability at the present time, reserve backing for production is such that sufficiency cannot be sustained in the long run. Even with increased production activity in 1979–1980 caused by the NGPA, reserve / production ratios did not materially improve and reserve additions continued to lag behind production. Given a continued reserve shortage, there is a potential for a deliverability shortage in the middle 1980s. With a continuation of NGPA controls in their present form, a substantial "price spike" will be required to rid the market of the shortages. Moreover, there are serious adverse distributional effects from continuing the NGPA in its present form. The impact of the "spike" on the various

39. Russell, "Natural Gas Deregulation," p. 18.

TABLE 19 *Forecast Supply and Demand with Constant Prices (trillion cubic feet)*

	Supply	Demand
1981 Actual	18.76	18.76
1982 Forecast	19.03	17.65
1983 Forecast	19.20	18.11
1984 Forecast	19.12	18.90
1985 Forecast	18.84	19.93

SOURCES: 1981 actual supply and demand from "The Current State of the Natural Gas Market; An Analysis of the Natural Gas Policy Act and Several Alternatives, Part I" DOE/EIA–0313, December 1981, p.41.

Forecast demands are as estimated from the simple growth function

$$\frac{\Delta D(t)}{D(t)} = \epsilon_I \left(\frac{\Delta income}{income} \right) + \epsilon_{p\ oil} \left(\frac{\Delta price\ oil}{price\ oil} \right) + \epsilon_{p\ gas} \left(\frac{\Delta price\ gas}{price\ gas} \right) + \gamma \left(\frac{\Delta D(t-1)}{D(t-1)} \right)$$

where Δ is change, ϵ is the elasticity, γ is the coefficient of lagged demand,[a] and $D(t)$ is demand in the year t.

Demand Equation Assumptions: $\Delta income/income$ = % change in GNP, DRI forecast;[b] $\Delta price\ oil/price\ oil$ = 0% average over 4 years; $\Delta price\ gas/price\ gas$ = 0%. The following elasticities and lagged demand coefficients were measured using regression analysis on demand and price date for 1978–1982 from the *Monthly Energy Review* (DOE/EIA 0035):

	Residential/ commercial	Industrial	Electric utility	Transpor- tation
Gas price elasticity	–.11	–.13	–.11	–.20
Income elasticity	.65	.32	.48	0
Oil price elasticity	.05	0	.11	.2
Coefficient of lagged demand	.79	0	.58	.60

TABLE 19 (*Continued*)

Forecast supplies are estimated from the functions

$$S(t) = reserves\ (t-1) \times [1 - \exp(-P/R)] + new\ development\ well\ production\ (t)$$

$$Reserves\ (t) = reserves\ (t-1) + new\ discoveries\ (t) - supply\ (t-1)$$

$$New\ discoveries\ (t) = find\ rate \times total\ drilling\ (t)$$

$$\frac{\Delta total\ drilling\ (t)}{total\ drilling\ (t)} = \epsilon_P \left(\frac{\Delta price\ (t)}{price\ (t)} \right) + \epsilon_C \left(\frac{\Delta drilling\ costs\ (t)}{drilling\ costs\ (t)} \right) + \gamma \left(\frac{\Delta total\ drilling\ (t-1)}{total\ drilling\ (t-1)} \right)$$

$Find\ rate\ (t) = d + ax \exp[-b \times cumulative\ drilling\ (t)]$

where Δ is change, ϵ is the elasticity, γ is the coefficient of lagged supply, and $S(t)$ is the supply in year t.

Supply Equations Assumptions: The following elasticities and lagged demand coefficients were measured using regression analysis on drilling and price data for 1958–1981 from the American Petroleum Institute:

	Developmental drilling	New field exploratory drilling	Other exploratory drilling
Gas price elasticity	.38	.10	.18
Cost elasticity	-.001	-.002	-.026
Coefficient of lagged demand	.41	.71	.61

These equations produce forecasts of excess supply for 1983–1984. But given NGPA partial decontrol, they were solved for the equilibrium condition, *Demand* = *Supply*, in the years after 1985.

[a]For a more complete description of the lagged adjustment process, see Paul W. MacAvoy, *Crude Oil Prices: As Determined by OPEC and Market Fundamentals* (Cambridge, Mass.: Ballinger, 1982), p. 26, note 8.

[b]Data Resources, Inc. *An Analysis of the Macroeconomic, Price and Consumption Impacts of the Proposed Administrative Action to Increase the Price of Selected Categories of Natural Gas*, August 26, 1982, p. 72: 1982 = -1.17, 1983 = 2.89, 1984 = 4.17, 1985 = 4.37.

TABLE 20 *Forecasts of Prices and Quantities of Domestic Natural Gas in the Middle 1980s*

Year	Average domestic price[a]	% change	Marketed production[b]	Demand for marketed production[b]
1981	2.32		18.76	18.76
1982	2.61	12.5	19.09	17.65
1983	2.69	2.9	19.44	18.16
1984	2.68	−0.3	19.63	19.08
1985	3.20	19.3	19.71	19.71
1986	3.83	19.8	20.15	20.15
1987	4.33	13.1	20.78	20.78

[a] In 1981 dollars per 1000 cubic feet.

[b] In trillions of cubic feet.

SOURCE: As described in the text, for the case of continued NGPA controls.

pipelines and retail distributors will be different in each case. With more price increases in the interim on old gas, the sharpness of the spike in 1985 could be moderated and even eliminated. But as regulation now stands, artificial inducements to demand growth and decontrol will come together to cause the maximum disruption in consumer markets.

Summary

The NGPA as designed by Congress did not solve but rather institutionalized the problems in gas controls. But given also an incorrect forecast for oil prices in setting out the new gas-price policy, the size of the price increase at the time of decontrol will likely exceed that envisioned at the time the legislation was passed. With phased gas price increases too low as compared to world crude price increases, the act could make "transitional deregulation" worse than the regulatory status quo of 1978. The only favorable attribute of the act is its devotion to home consumers. The two-price system of NGPA resale controls would have household users pay a lower price than industrial users in wholesale markets.[40] The industrial and residential markets continue to be kept apart by this new policy, even after 1985, to protect residential buyers from the price competition by industry seeking this choice source of energy for process use.

Whether this is equitable cannot be determined, since the loss of gas to industry changes the prices and quantities of final goods in ways adverse at least to some home consumers. But the NGPA did not meet the standards set out for reform. By keeping gas prices low to residential users, by using up the "bubble" to meet increased demands fostered by low prices, and by forcing industry to higher cost fuel oil, the policy has wasted resources. The NGPA

40. These prices were equivalent in the early 1960s, once account was taken of cost of delivery differences and demand elasticity differences (Paul W. MacAvoy and Roger Noll, "Relative Prices on Regulated Transactions of the Natural Gas Pipelines," *Bell Journal of Economics and Management Science* 4 [1973]: 212).

concern not for efficiency but for equity in the use of natural gas resources has created massive equity problems for the future. When controls are phased out in the 1980s the price shocks may well be more "unfair" than would have been those from complete decontrol in 1980. Thus natural gas regulation has created mixed results. While the goal of income redistribution might be said to have been achieved, if only for those not experiencing shortages, it is likely that the problems fostered by the NGPA will totally undo these effects with decontrol as planned. In addition, conditions of supply stringency, allocative inefficiency, and increased embargo vulnerability due to growing industrial reliance on oil persist. The gas policy of the 1970s succeeded only in perpetuating the costs of, and perhaps even indecision on, decontrol.

4

◇◇◇◇◇

Service Quality and Regulation in Retail
Electricity and Gas

The ELECTRIC AND GAS utility companies set the pace for industrial growth and performance in the 1950s and early 1960s. No other industry provided services more widely, or with greater regularity and promptness to residential and industrial customers. Gas distributors promised the cheapest and cleanest home heating and cooking fuel while the electrics stressed their falling prices and unfailing service in meeting the demands of both old and new customers.

By the start of the 1970s, however, these retail energy companies were in trouble: rates were increasing, the quality of existing service was deteriorating, and availability of new service was being restricted for the first time in some localities. Rather than extolling their dedication to service, the corporations more often apologized for delays and shortages, and urged the consumer to conserve gas or electricity.

Why the reversal in a single decade? Consumer groups blamed the regulated companies for laxness in controlling costs, for mistakes in adopting new technologies, and for passing on to customers the costs of these mistakes. In reply the companies pointed to increased inflation and reduced productivity growth, but principally they blamed their declining performance on the failures of regulation. Indeed both critics and producers criticized the regulators for imposing controls that were time-consuming, costly, and most often mistaken in their basic decisions. The agencies in turn maintained that legislative mandates required procedures or decisions that caused perverse results in the new economic conditions of the 1970s.

Since the regulated electric and gas utilities provide the infrastructure for delivering an important part of energy supplies throughout the national economy, it is important to determine which of these explanations for the declines in service are correct. To this end, we first describe the regulatory process and show how it affects public utility company price and output decisions. The effects of regulation on the electric and gas companies from 1958 to the present are shown by documenting the direction and magnitudes of changes in service quality, and then determining the extent to which these changes can be attributed to the operations of the agencies. During the first third of this period, from 1958 to 1965, economic conditions and regulations produced beneficial results; during the 1965–1979 period, however, markedly different economic conditions combined with the same regulatory conditions to generate quite contradictory and much more adverse results.

Making such a detailed assessment of the impact of utility regulation requires evaluation of the regulation's purposes, the government's success in achieving those objectives, and the added costs imposed by the regulation.

In electric power and gas distribution, conditions of natural monopoly create an environment conducive to government regulation. Due to economies of scale arising from declining average costs, a single large firm can price lower than any set of smaller firms. To prevent the abuse of market power by the natural monopolist, government has two options: to supervise the monopolist or to break it up into competing firms. The second option is economically undesirable because it does not permit utilities to obtain the lowest cost level of production. Thus government intervention takes the form of regulating the monopolist primarily to prevent higher than competitive prices and to ensure universal service.

Is government successful in meeting these goals? And what costs are involved? The discussion that follows examines public utility rate-setting practices of the last few years and their consequences for electric power and gas industry price levels, supply availability, and—an additional factor especially important here—quality of service.

The Regulatory Process

Despite differences in statute mandates and industries, the public utility commissions have operated in roughly similar ways and thus had developed certain common authority over the 1940s and 1950s. Through rule making and case-by-case review they have approved company applications for service. They have allowed price increases based on findings that these increases were in line with increased costs as measured in accounting terms. The company in turn has selected its own production methods and determined its capacity to supply consumers in designated or certified markets.

Similarities exist not only in what regulatory agencies control, but also in the decision processes used. Initially agencies issue "certificates" to companies selected to provide service across regions, to different classifications of consumers, and for particular time periods. Commissions have, for example, established the number of electric companies to serve a region, designated classes of industrial, as contrasted with residential, consumers, and set service standards for peak demands as well as for annual operations.

The most important practices have been those used to set price levels.[1] The first step has been to certify tariffs submitted to establish prices or "rates" on scheduled service. But rather than investigating thousands of rate schedules of any one company, the

1. Controls on market entry and exit are also important, of course. They are found in conjunction with price regulations, however, so the effects of nonprice economic regulations can be incorporated into those attributable to price controls.

regulatory commissions have allowed company requests for general revenue increases, and have supplemented them with directions as to how to parcel out allowed revenue increases among the individual service tariffs. The agencies evaluate requests based on evidence of increased operating costs, higher depreciation allowances, and increases in the capital returns required by bond- and stockholders.

The central issue in a decision has been whether companies would be earning excess profits from revenue or price increases. Company returns should be just sufficient to attract investors, and thereby to sustain current and prospective increased inflows of capital necessary to maintain and expand service. Thus any proposed increases in revenues are measured against the standard of a "fair" rate of return on a level of capital "rate base."

In using this standard, agencies have employed measures of investment or "rate base" that include expenditures on plant and equipment used in regulated operations, estimated by their original costs less depreciation. The agencies have set the "fair" rate of return on this base customarily within a range, based on evidence and judgment on what the company has to earn to compete successfully for funds required to replace and, if necessary, expand capacity. Since these funds must be obtained from prospective debt and equity holders, the determination has centered on what companies have to pay in interest, dividends, and (implicitly) stock price appreciation to maintain a competitive level of borrowings and equity investment. This can be and indeed has been quite subjective. The competitive rate of return on equity capital cannot be estimated, as one might expect, from recent ratios of dividends to stock prices because investors' expectations of the future rate of growth of dividends affects the current level of any stock price. But such ratios and judgments of experts on capital returns are used by the agencies to set a ceiling on allowed rates of return.

With rapidly changing economic conditions, the agencies have often erred in their findings on required levels of profit and interest returns. Given the high degree of subjectivity, they end up by choosing what other agencies have allowed and by following behind large increases or decreases in government bond interest rates. During the late 1960s and the early 1970s in particular, the process resulted in downward-biased estimates of required revenue increases. This was at least partly the result of repeated use of the established administrative processes. Under conditions of rising rates of inflation, the conventional review would use past statistics that underestimated the current replacement cost of capital and the current earned rates of return on other investments. Also, the bias increased after regulatory proceedings were widened to allow access as intervenors to self-proclaimed "consumer" groups resisting rate increases. These groups, and other intervenors representing industrial or commercial buyers of regulated services, presented data and testimony that favored too-low estimates of increased capital costs. They carried political weight in the proceedings, regardless of the content in their estimates, and the process of splitting differences between them and company estimates resulted in inadequate allowed returns.

The regulated firms responded with a deluge of additional requests for further revenue increases. This led to more frequent rate proceedings, which the agencies attempted to deal with through more comprehensive and thus more prolonged reviews. In the presence of large and growing requests, these investigations placed more weight on the intervenors' case for low prices. So in an effort to stem the flood of litigation on both sides, the commissions finally began to permit substantial increases, but still held average allowed rates of return two or three percentage points below those on comparable alternative investments.

The importance of the political and inflation factors was apparent in the New York regulatory experience. During the late 1960s and early 1970s the electric power companies requested increases whenever in the presence of advancing inflation their rates of return on investment fell substantially below those of previous years. They requested additional revenues when the growth rate of earnings per share declined or when interest coverage fell (that is, when after-tax income as a proportion of interest was reduced). The companies also entered larger revenue requests after the commission had permitted larger increases to other firms. But the actual New York case decisions showed that the commission specifically downgraded the amount of the company's request in the presence of intervenors.[2]

Although not all state and federal agencies followed the particular practices of the New York commission, most considered and weighted these price-stabilizing factors. On the whole they allowed increases in revenues to take account of rising raw material and direct energy costs. Further increases, however, fell short of capital cost changes for long periods of time during the late 1960s and the 1970s. Only when requests were made by most of the regulated companies at the same time, so that the case load became "stacked," did the regulatory agencies tend to approve requests for significantly higher revenues and thus higher rates of return. The commissions, otherwise besieged by contention, allowed too little and too late.

Regulatory Effects on Service Quality

These controls as a matter of course had widespread and significant effects not only on price levels but also on service offerings.

When the economy was growing rapidly and inflation rates were low, cost increases were limited, so that the regulated companies did not have to seek revenue increases to make adequate profit margins on expanded service. Further, system expansion permitted the realization of economies of scale which when combined with improved technology brought about reduced unit costs of providing service. With constant price levels and falling unit costs, the companies in fact were able to generate higher profit margins on larger volumes of service. Such improved profit opportunities

2. Paul L. Joskow, "Pricing Decisions of Regulated Firms: A Behavioral Approach," *Bell Journal of Economics and Management Science* 4 (Autumn 1973): 118–40; and Paul L. Joskow, "The Determination of the Allowed Rate of Return in a Formal Regulatory Hearing," *Bell Journal of Economics and Management Science* 3 (Autumn 1972): 632–44.

were an added inducement to new investment which in turn improved the quantity and quality of service.

But during periods of high inflation and low demand growth, prices fell behind costs and the regulated companies' revenues were not sufficient to provide for equipment replacement and capacity expansion. Slower economic growth reduced capacity utilization, thereby increasing the fixed-cost burden per unit of output. This burden was quite particular to these regulated companies, since their future prices depended on their present unit costs. Inflation in the prices for plant, equipment, and material used in producing these services further raised unit costs. The companies then went to the commissions seeking revenue increases, and received in response allowances that did not cover the cost increases. Without a sufficient increase in revenues, the regulated company realized lower profits, which reduced the capital market value of the firm's securities. The regulated companies then had to reduce both internally and externally financed capital outlays, which reduced the capacity to serve current and prospective customers. Just as the regulatory process amplified the effect of a healthy economy on regulated firms, it made inflation more acutely adverse to service growth in these industries than elsewhere in the economy.

In fact the second set of conditions dominated the performance of the regulated gas and electric companies in the late 1960s and the 1970s. Costs were increasing and the state regulatory agencies were newly occupied with the political effects of rate increases. The agencies granted insufficient revenue increases relative to the cost of providing existing levels of service, and they continued to delay firms' requests even when making these grants. As a result sequential reductions took place in investment and, in the end, in service quality. This cost-price-profit-investment-service "nexus" was the result of the prevailing regulatory process and it determined the performance of the regulated companies through the entire 1970s.[3]

3. It might be argued that the higher levels of service quality prevailing in the 1960s were excessive, and that the increased stringency of rate control has now

The Growth of Service, 1958–1965

In the late 1950s the economy entered a period of sustained growth and low inflation. Real gross national product (GNP), which had increased at a 2.1 percent annual rate during 1952–1958, grew 3.6 percent annually from 1958 to 1961, and then 5.2 percent a year until 1965. The inflation rate did not exceed 2 percent through most of the 1952–1965 period. Interest rates on three-month Treasury bills rose only gradually, from 2 percent in the early 1950s to 3 percent in the early 1960s.[4] This record set high standards, and indeed it turned out to be twice the growth rate but no more than one-third the inflation rate experienced over any sustained period in the late 1960s and the 1970s.

The electricity-generating and gas-distributing industries participated in and contributed to the surpassing performance of the economy at that time. To a measurable extent, high rates of growth in manufacturing and housing required large and sustained increases in service from these public utilities. Service demands were met by expanding capacity which in turn increased productivity.

The companies in these two industries experienced labor pro-

---

returned these industries to a more desirable quality level. At issue is the appropriate level of service. Optimal service quality may be defined simply as that level for which the additional willingness to pay (marginal revenue) equals the marginal costs of providing the extra quality of service. Studies indicating the existence in the 1960s of excess service quality as measured in these terms are few. Those that exist are confined to the airline passenger service industry, characterized by extensive interairline service competition. One might expect to encounter more studies in electricity and gas like that of Douglas and Miller on the airlines, but even they found higher service quality to be confined to a few markets with excessively wide price-cost margins (where service dissipates the excess profits). Cf. George W. Douglas and James C. Miller III, *Economic Regulation of Domestic Air Transport* (Washington, D.C.: Brookings Institution, 1974), pp. 68–75. Thus the declines of service quality in the 1970s were probably moving the industries away from and not toward the optimal level.

4. *Economic Report of the President* (January 1979), Table B–2, "Gross National Product in 1972 Dollars, 1929–78," p. 184; Table B–3, "Implicit Price Deflator for Gross National Product, 1929–78," p. 186; and Table B–65, "Bond Yields and Interest Rates, 1929–78," p. 258.

ductivity increases that exceeded those of the rest of the economy over the 1958–1965 period (see Table 21). Such high productivity growth came from numerous and diverse sources, but scale and technology were most important. Economies of scale were present in the electric power industry on both the plant and distribution system levels. As the size of generating units increased, production costs per kilowatt-hour declined, and as firms expanded their transmission facilities, these unit costs also decreased. At the same time the larger plants and improvements in the technology for shifting power within a region enabled the industry to pool capacity so as to reduce the size of reserve equipment held against plant failure or unduly high peak demands. Similarly, systems growth led to productivity gains in the natural gas industry. Gas pipeline transmission and retail distribution benefited from increasing returns to more complete utilization of the large pipelines installed in the early and middle 1950s.[5]

The productivity gains kept the regulated industries ahead of their wage and capital cost increases. In some cases productivity growth exceeded factor cost increases so that the public utilities realized reductions in current costs of producing and delivering services. This implied that prices could be reduced, or at least

5. These have been termed "economies of massed reserves." See E. A. G. Robinson, *The Structure of Competitive Industry* (rev. ed.; Chicago: University of Chicago Press, 1958), pp. 26–77. Changes in technology also resulted in more capital-intensive, more fuel-intensive, and hence more productive operations (when measured by output per man-hour); stable real prices for capital inputs and falling real prices for fuel encouraged this form of input substitution. See Stephen G. Breyer and Paul W. MacAvoy, "The Federal Power Commission and the Coordination Problem in the Electrical Power Industry," *Southern California Law Review* 46, no. 3 (June 1973): 664–70; and W. R. Hughes, "Short-Run Efficiency and the Organization of the Electric Power Industry," *Quarterly Journal of Economics* 76, no. 4 (November 1962: 592–612. Economies of scale in gas transmission are a function of the "two-thirds power rule," by which costs increase slightly more than proportionately to diameter but capacity increases by more than the square of diameter. See Paul W. MacAvoy, *Price Formation in Natural Gas Fields* (New Haven: Yale University Press, 1962), pp. 37–41. Until 1965 production increased more rapidly than capacity; thereafter, capacity was added more rapidly than throughput, thereby reducing capacity utilization. Thus productivity growth slowed in the late 1960s.

TABLE 21 *Productivity Changes in the Regulated Energy Industries, 1958–1965*[a]

Industry	1958–1961	1961–1965
Electric	5.5	5.6
Natural gas	7.0	7.6
Other regulated service industries (telephone)	7.8	5.4
Private domestic economy[b]	2.6	4.0

[a] % average annual rate of change in output per man-hour. *Note:* Unless otherwise indicated the industry groupings used in this and subsequent tables are those of the Department of Commerce Standard Industrial Classification (SIC) system: Electric (generation and distribution, SIC 491). Where shown, "unregulated services" include the following components of SIC 50–90: wholesale and retail trade; insurance agents, brokers, services; hotels and other lodging places; personal services; miscellaneous business services; auto repair, services, garages; miscellaneous repair services; motion pictures; amusement, recreation services; educational services.

[b] Including the regulated industries given above.

SOURCES: U.S. Department of Labor, Bureau of Labor Statistics, Office of Economic Growth, unpublished data (November 1977).

held constant, while service offerings were increased. Whether they were reduced or held constant depended on how the regulatory authorities behaved[6] (see Table 22).

The companies in fact made infrequent requests of the regulatory agencies for revenue changes (see Table 23). In fact prices decreased in these industries between 1961 and 1965 while those elsewhere in the economy rose by two percentage points per year (as in Table 24). Commission-requested and voluntary price reductions brought about between a third of a point and a half-point annual decline in regulated price levels, even though costs were increasing slightly in spite of the aforementioned rapid growth of productivity.

This combination of expansive business cycle conditions and rate level freeze seems to have resulted in modest if not disappointing profit returns to holders of the regulated companies' debt and equity. The profit experience is shown in Table 25, with both realized rates of return in these industries and alternative investment returns to stockholders for the early 1960s. The indication from these estimates is that the companies did not provide in interest, dividends, and stock price appreciation more than what was earned on investments of comparable risk in other industries. With less than expected returns in gas company investments, but with more than expected returns in electric company shares, a portfolio of investments in regulated energy companies did neither better nor worse than one containing companies elsewhere in the economy.

Who then gained from increased productivity? During this period the commissions and the regulated companies increasingly employed rate structures and service offerings that would promote more rapid industry expansion. Demand increases and cost reduc-

6. It should be noted that the productivity indices arguably may be biased by changes in input or output mix. Criticisms have also been leveled against the methodology employed in the Bureau of Labor Statistics data series, particularly with regard to the output calculations. Using a different approach, Gollop and Jorgenson have calculated total factor productivity measures for the regulated industries under study. As shown in Table 22, their results generally confirm the patterns presented in Table 21.

TABLE 22 *Total Factor Productivity in the Regulated Industries, 1957–1966[a]*

Industry	1957–1960	1960–1966
Electric	3.96	2.07
Natural gas	−1.46	1.82
Other regulated (telephone)	3.08	2.17
Unregulated services	0.23	1.10
Total U.S. economy	−0.49	1.19

[a] % average annual rate of change.

SOURCE: Frank M. Gollop and Dale Jorgenson, "U.S. Productivity Growth by Industry, 1947–73," Discussion Paper No. 570, Harvard Institute of Economic Research, September 1977.

TABLE 23 *Electric and Gas Rate Case Proceedings, 1962–1965*

| Industry | Average number of new proceedings | | Allowed revenue changes per year (millions of dollars) | |
	Per year	% change from 1959–1961 to 1962–1965	Increases	Decreases
Electric	63	−14.3	14.3	42.7
Natural gas	64	−16.6	17.5	21.9

SOURCE: EBASCO Investor-Owned Utility Rate Decisions, Increases and Decreases Granted and Pending, 1978, State or Local Jurisdiction.

TABLE 24 *Prices and Costs in the Regulated Energy Industries, 1961–1965*[a]

Industry	Unit prices	Unit costs[b]
Electric	−0.3	0.6
Natural gas	−0.5	0.1
Total price regulated (includes telephone, airline, and railroad)	−0.5	0.7
Unregulated services	1.8	1.7
Total U.S. economy	1.8	0.9

[a]% average annual rate of change.

[b]Unit costs C are calculated from the changes in unit prices P and sales price-cost margins, according to the following formula:

$$(C_t)/(C_v) = [(P_t/P_v)(1 - S_t/1 - S_v)]$$

where t denotes the current year's data, v denotes the base year's data, and S is the ratio of net income to gross revenues. The resulting tabulations are then annualized. Calculations for this period and subsequent periods based on a weighted average of input-cost changes yielded results consistent with those reported here. See Paul W. MacAvoy, *The Regulated Industries and the Economy* (New York: W. W. Norton, 1979), pp. 72, 136–37.

SOURCES: U.S. Department of Labor, Bureau of Labor Statistics, unpublished data (1979); Standard & Poor's Corp., Compustat (1979).

TABLE 25 *Profitability of the Regulated Energy Industries, 1961–1965*[a]

Industry	Actual return	Market equivalent return[c]	Difference[d]
Electric	5.9	5.1	+0.8
Gas transmission	4.3	7.7	−3.4
Gas utility	5.4	5.6	−0.2
Unregulated services	7.4	10.9	−3.5
Market total[b]	8.2	—	—

[a] % average of annual rates of return on investors' value. *Note:* "Rate of return on investors' value" is the market value-weighted average of interest, dividends, and stock price appreciation divided by the market value of all securities for that industry.

[b] Composite return for approximately 1400 publicly traded firms. Market equivalent return equals actual return for market total, by definition.

[c] Stock market and bond market returns are derived by adjusted industry-specific risk premium (Beta).

[d] Actual return less market equivalent return. A positive difference is a measure of the extent to which investors were overcompensated for the riskiness of the particular investment.

SOURCE: Author's calculations based on Standard & Poor's Compustat (1978). For a description of the methodology used, see Paul W. MacAvoy, *The Regulated Industries and the Economy* (New York: W. W. Norton, 1979), Appendix D.

tions were allowed under regulation to yield profit returns only sufficient to induce further investment to improve services for final consumers.

The result was that in 1958–1965 the quantity of service expanded and service reliability held steady at a high level (see Table 26).[7] Electric power shortages were few, and those that did occur resulted from unexpected weather damage rather than from shortages of generating capacity. In the natural gas industry, reserve backing for the production and delivery of gas by the interstate pipelines was falling but the reliability of gas deliveries was not affected. At the same time, investment, capacity, and ultimately the volume of service offered to consumers grew rapidly, generally exceeding that of the manufacturing sector (as in Table 27). The growth rate of production exceeded that of the general economy by at least two percentage points a year over the 1958–1961 period. Again, during 1961–1965 the production growth rate in the regulated power industry exceeded that of the economy, and that of the gas industry matched that of the economy, even though the economy's growth rate had increased by two points over the earlier period (as in Table 28).

By the mid-1960s the pattern of service performance had become clearly established. Regulation and industry cost reductions had caused prices for public utility services to fall relative to those in the unregulated service industries. Falling relative prices induced increases in per-capita consumption of regulated services exceeding those in the rest of the economy. Service offerings expanded to meet these demands, both in quality and quantity, partly because specific regulatory policies encourage such expansion.

7. Measures of service quality have been developed here for the regulated industries in an attempt to capture more of the attributes of these services than are apparent in the data on output quantities. In compiling two indicators for each industry, we have tried to evaluate the service intended to be offered—electric reserves—and the realized quality levels. In some cases the measures approach closely the ideal indicators of quality; in others the lack of suitable data forces the use of less precise or accurate indices. The index numbers should be analyzed for the direction of change and the level relative to the base year. Less importance should be attached to comparison of magnitudes across industries, given the diversity of the indicators and the resulting indexation.

136

TABLE 26 *Service Quality in the Regulated Energy Industries, 1958–1965*

Industry / Index[a]	1961	1965
Electricity		
Expected capability margin	144	109
Natural gas		
Reserve capacity	90	84
Curtailments	100	100

[a]Higher index indicates improved service; service quality index, 1958 = 100.

SOURCES: Service quality indices are the author's calculations, based on industry and government data, adjusted for comparability. *Electric*: Gross reserve margin at peak, excess of actual capacity over demand in marker year predicted at the time of the capacity decision, Edison Electric Institute, *Electric Power Survey* (various years). Electric utility outages and load reductions (except storm related) relative to electricity consumption, Federal Power Commission, quarterly news releases (various years); U.S. Department of Energy, "Statistics of Electric Utilities in the United States" (various issues). *Natural Gas*: Ratio of natural gas reserves to annual gross production, American Gas Association, *Gas Facts* (1978); ratio of natural gas curtailments to annual sales, Federal Power Commission/Federal Energy Regulatory Commission, ad hoc special reports and Form 16 Reports of Gas Supply and Requirements (various years).

TABLE 27 *Investment and Capacity Growth in the Regulated Energy Industries, 1958–1965*

Industry	Measure (source)	1958–1961[a]	1961–1965[a]
Electric	Net capital stock (BEA)	5.3	4.1
Gas transmission	Net capital stock (BLS)	4.0	3.1
Manufacturing	Net capital stock (BEA)	0.3	2.4
Total U.S. economy	Net capital stock (BEA)	2.8	4.2

[a] % average annual rate of change.

SOURCES: U.S. Department of Commerce, Bureau of Economic Analysis (BEA); U.S. Department of Labor, Bureau of Labor Statistics (BLS).

TABLE 28   *Rates of Output Growth in the Regulated Industries, 1958–1965* [a]

Industry	1958–1961 [b]	1961–1965 [b]
Electric	5.5	7.2
Natural gas	5.8	5.6
Unregulated services	2.9	5.1
Total U.S. economy	3.6	5.2

[a] Output growth is measured in terms of real gross national product.

[b] % average annual rate of change.

SOURCES: U.S. Department of Labor, Bureau of Labor Statistics, unpublished data (1978); *Economic Report of the President* (January 1979).

Promotional Rate Structures

The thousands of different prices that made up "rate structure" for regulated services vary one from the other because of differences in costs related to distance, volume of purchases, time of day, season, and the specific quality of services. Beyond variation with costs, the structure varied with demand conditions, particularly those related to the presence or absence of alternative energy services.[8] But the regulatory agencies exercised control over the rate structure by issuing standards for determining the range of rates, and by directly setting the rates for some specific services while still controlling overall revenues.

A number of different goals for rate structures were pursued, not always in a consistent or exact way. But an important element of regulated rate policy was to achieve "value-of-service" pricing in which lower rates were to be quoted to those classes of customers with high price elasticity of demand. This scheme permitted greater growth in sales than a completely cost-based rate structure would have.[9] Further in that direction, in the 1960s the agencies kept certain rates down so as to expand service demands of favored

8. Evaluation of cost allocation issues in the regulated industries presents a number of theoretical and methodological problems. The electric, natural gas, and (to a lesser degree) other regulated retail service companies exhibit aspects of a natural monopoly. Marginal-cost pricing is efficient but leads to losses at all levels of output because average costs exceed marginal costs for all relevant levels of demand. Possible solutions are average-cost pricing, price discrimination, or external subsidies. Thus a pricing structure that shows prices diverging from incremental costs may be a response to natural monopoly, an explicit income redistribution scheme, or a combination of the two. A closely related problem is the peak-load issue. For industries that must build a large capital plant to handle the maximum demand over a cycle (and in which output cannot be stored), there is the question of how to allocate the fixed costs. At peak utilization the marginal cost to serve an additional customer includes additional capital stock; during off-peak times there are only the variable costs. Average-cost pricing, or even a system with higher rates for peak service, may involve smaller price-cost margins for peak users than for off-peak users.

9. See W. J. Baumol and D. F. Bradford, "Optimal Departures from Marginal Cost Pricing," *American Economic Review* 60 (June 1970).

consumers. For example, some agencies pressed the utilities serving large geographic areas to charge all subscribers the same monthly rate for service, even though it was more costly to serve smaller or more remote subscribers. These exceptions created rate disparity beyond that found in any strict value-of-service schedule.

This sometimes led to cross-subsidization, or subsidization of one service by excess profits on another. By the early 1960s the electric utilities offered fairly wide schedules of rates that would encourage customers to install electric heating, cooling, and hot water systems.[10] Gas distribution companies, faced with rising prices for wholesale gas from the interstate pipelines, were generally advised by state public utility commissions to freeze residential rates but increase industrial and commercial rates.[11] In fact, both industrial gas and electricity rates increased more than rates to residential consumers except where lower industrial power rates permitted realization of economies of scale which served in turn to reduce rates for home customers.[12]

10. These services, competitive with those based on fuel oil and natural gas, were clearly more price elastic. For a more complete description of the motivations for cross-subsidization in electric power, see H. Bierman, Jr., and J. E. Hass, "Inflation, Equity, Efficiency and the Regulatory Pricing of Electricity," *Public Policy* 23, no. 3 (Summer 1975): 303; J. P. Blair, "The Politics of Government Pricing: Political Influences on the Rate Structure of Publicly-Owned Electric Utilities," *American Journal of Economics and Sociology* 35, no. 1 (January 1976); Sam Peltzman, "Pricing in Public and Private Enterprises: Electric Utilities in the United States," *Journal of Law and Economics* 14 (April 1971): 109–49; and H. W. Pifer and E. L. Scholl, "An Analysis of Recent Electric Utility Rate Increases," Temple, Barker, and Sloane, Inc., the Energy and Environment Group (June 1975).

11. See A. C. Aman and G. S. Howard, "Natural Gas and Electric Utility Rate Reform: Taxation Through Rate-Making," *Hastings Law Journal* 28, no. 5 (1977); and S. Wellisz, "The Public Interest in Gas Industry Rate Structure," *Public Utilities Fortnightly* 70 (July 19, 1962).

12. Cf. A. S. Carron and P. W. MacAvoy, *The Decline of Service in the Regulated Industries* (Washington, D.C.: American Enterprise Institute, 1981), Table 10, p. 31.

Regulation and Declining Service Quality in the 1970s

After 1965 an increasingly inhospitable economic climate combined with regulation to erode growth and service quality in the public utility and transportation sector. By all measures the national economy did not perform as well after 1965 as it did in the first half of the decade. Real GNP growth fell from an average annual rate of slightly more than 5 percent in 1961–1965 to slightly less than 4 percent in 1965–1969. At the same time the annual rate of increase in the GNP price deflator more than doubled from 1.8 percent to 3.9 percent. Interest rates, as represented by three-month Treasury bills, also more than doubled, rising from 2.9 percent in 1960 to 6.7 percent a year in 1969, effectively cutting business investment by one-half.[13]

This new path for the economy had a major effect on behavior in the regulated industries. The slower rate of economywide growth led to reduced rates of demand growth for utility services. Smaller increments of demand required more limited additions to capacity, so that it took the electric and gas industries longer to install new technology. As a result the regulated industries experienced lower rates of productivity growth and, with rising wage rates and capital and fuel costs, production costs began to rise rapidly.

With greater cost inflation at hand, the companies submitted numerous and large requests for rate increases to the regulatory agencies each year. Faced with these cases, the regulatory agencies acted frequently and diligently, but still failed to approve increases large enough to keep up with service cost increases. The case decisions kept average price increases at a fraction of that for the economy as a whole, and also well below the cost increases actually realized in these industries (see Table 29).

Those quite limited increases in regulated prices during 1965–

13. *Economic Report of the President* (January 1979), Table B–2, "Gross National Product in 1972 Dollars, 1929–78"; Table B–3, "Implicit Price Deflations for Gross National Product, 1929–78"; and Table B–65, "Bond Yields and Interest Rates, 1929–78."

TABLE 29 *Prices and Costs in the Regulated Energy Industries, 1965–1969*[a]

Industry	Unit prices	Unit costs[b]
Electric	0.5	2.3
Natural gas	0.1	0.7
Other regulated (includes telephone, airline, and railroad)	0.7	2.9
Unregulated service industries	4.5	4.4
Total U.S. economy	3.4	3.0

[a] % average annual rate of change.

[b] See Table 24.

SOURCES: U.S. Department of Labor, Bureau of Labor Statistics, unpublished data (1979); Standard & Poor's Compustat (1979).

1969 in turn reduced operating profit margins and subsequently the profits on investment in the public utilities. Lower profits were reflected in reduced stock market valuation for the electric and gas companies (see Table 30) so that stockholders earned less than half the market rate of return (except in the gas transmission industry, where economies of fuller utilization of existing plant were still being realized to such an extent that unit costs were not increasing; even here, however, returns were below alternative investment returns). A somewhat improved profit performance of regulated energy industries in the 1969–1973 period was not sufficient to offset the poor returns of 1965–1969, and for the eight-year period as a whole returns adjusted for risk were below the market rate (see Table 31).

Such were the steps that led to the downgrading of performance in the regulated industries in the 1970s. The economic conditions prevailing at the beginning of the decade were not favorable. During 1969–1973 real GNP growth fell by half a percentage point, while the GNP price deflator went up by more than one percentage point. Over the following five years real GNP growth fell an additional percentage point, from 3.4 percent in 1969–1973 to 2.3 percent in 1973–1978. The price deflator rose at an average annual rate of 3.9 percent in 1965–1969, 5.1 percent a year in 1969–1973, and then 7.5 percent a year in 1973–1978. The combination of continued inflationary expectations and restrictive monetary policy caused interest rates to increase from 5.0 percent over 1965–1969 to 5.7 percent in 1969–1973, and then to 6.4 percent in 1973–1978.[14] Partly because of these higher financing costs, investment growth fell to slightly more than 1 percent a year over the 1973–1978 period, thereby adding to the slowdown of productivity, capacity, and GNP growth.

The combination of lower growth and higher inflation spread to the regulated industries where reduced demand growth slowed down productivity growth, which, with higher factor prices, resulted in substantially greater increases in unit production costs.

14. This is the average interest rate on three-month Treasury bills; see *Economic Report of the President* (January 1979), Table B–65.

TABLE 30 Profitability of the Regulated Energy Industries, 1965–1980[a]

Industry	1965–1969			1969–1973			1973–1979			1979–1980		
	Actual return	Market equivalent return[c]	Difference[d]	Actual return	Market equivalent return[c]	Difference[d]	Actual return	Market equivalent return[c]	Difference[d]	Actual return	Market equivalent return[c]	Difference[d]
Electric	1.1	5.3	−4.2	5.5	5.1	+0.4	6.9	6.5	+0.4	8.2	11.2	−3.0
Gas transmission	3.7	5.2	−1.5	6.5	4.5	+2.0	10.2	6.3	+3.9	30.1	12.2	+17.9
Gas utility	1.8	5.3	−3.5	5.1	4.9	+0.2	8.0	6.5	+1.5	9.6	11.2	−1.6
Unregulated services	10.6	5.2	+5.4	2.2	3.7	−1.5	2.8	6.1	−3.3	11.8	11.3	+0.5
Market total[b]	5.2	—	—	4.4	—	—	6.1	—	—	11.5	—	—

[a] % average of annual rates of return. *Note:* "Rate of return on investors' value" is the market value-weighted average of interest, dividends, and stock price appreciation divided by the market value of all securities for that industry.

[b] Composite return for approximately 2400 publicly traded firms. Market equivalent return equals actual return for market total by definition.

[c] Stock market value of all securities for that industry.

[d] Actual return less market equivalent return. A positive difference is a measure of the extent to which investors are overcompensated for the riskiness of the particular investment.

SOURCE: Author's calculations based on Standard & Poor's Compustat (1980).

TABLE 31 *Electric and Gas Industry Rates of Return on Investors' Value, 1965–1973[a]*

Industry	Actual return	Equivalent market returns[b]
Electric	3.3	5.2
Gas transmission	5.1	4.9
Gas utility	3.4	5.1
Unregulated services	6.4	4.5
Market total	4.8	—

[a]% average of annual rates.

[b] As defined in Table 30.

SOURCE: Author's calculations based on Standard & Poor's Compustat (1978).

Lower demand growth also resulted in the regulated companies' having to spread high capital costs over smaller output for purposes of setting regulated rate levels. The combination of rising operating costs and rising overhead costs per unit of sales made the case for more revenue increases before the regulatory commissions.

The reduced productivity in the energy industries is indicated in Table 32. Between the early 1960s and 1970s productivity improvement rates fell by eight percentage points in the natural gas industry, principally because output was constrained by shortages in field supplies of gas. Productivity growth fell as well in the electric power industry, from 5 or 6 percent per year in the early 1960s to 4 percent a decade later.

One cause of reduced productivity growth was the lower rate of utilization of capacity, particularly new capacity, consequent from the economywide slowdown. These capital-intensive industries, which plan investment far in advance, were not able to adjust rapidly to a lower level of actual compared to forecast demand growth. Capacity utilization and growth rates both fell, making it difficult to capture efficiencies in newer technology.

But each of these regulated industries had reasons of its own for reduced productivity performance as well. During the middle and late 1950s new technology was not forthcoming in the electric power industry and scale economies were in large part exhausted at plant sizes of the early 1960s.[15] As fuel prices increased, labor-intensive technologies were more widely adopted and these by

15. L. Christensen and W. H. Greene, "Economies of Scale in U.S. Electric Power Generation," *Journal of Political Economy* 84 (1976): 655: "[I]n 1955 there were significant scale economies available to nearly all firms. By 1970, however, the bulk of U.S. electricity generation was by firms operating in the essentially flat area of the average cost curve." Lawrence W. Weiss, "Antitrust in the Electric Power Industry," in Almarin Phillips, ed., *Promoting Competition in Regulated Markets* (Washington, D.C.: Brookings Institution, 1975), p. 147: "The large increase in optimal scale relative to demand in the 1950s and 1960s will turn out to be a onetime change rather than trend." See also R. A. Nelson and M. E. Wohar, "Total Factor Productivity in the Electric Power Industry: A Disaggregated Approach" (Newark: University of Delaware, 1980), mimeographed.

TABLE 32 *Productivity Changes in the Regulated Energy Industries, 1961–1980*[a]

Industry	1961–1965	1965–1969	1969–1973	1973–1979	1979–1980
Electric	5.6	4.9	3.9	1.4	–3.5
Natural gas	7.6	5.3	–0.1	–0.7	1.8
Total U.S. economy	4.0	2.2	2.4	0.8	–0.2

[a]% average annual rate of change in output per man-hour.

SOURCES: U.S. Department of Labor, Bureau of Labor Statistics, unpublished data (June 1982); *Economic Report of the President* (February 1982), Table B-40; U.S. Department of Labor, Bureau of Labor Statistics, unpublished data (November 1979); *Economic Report of the President* (January 1979).

themselves caused lower labor productivity growth.[16] The impo-
sition of environmental and safety regulations on generating plants
in the late 1960s increased capital requirements without adding to
capacity, thereby reducing productivity growth. In natural gas,
the major reason was the wellhead shortage of gas that developed
in the early 1970s. Productivity declines in natural gas distribution resulted from the cutback in deliveries, or growth in deliveries, as stagnation in reserves committed to the interstate pipelines
set in during the late 1960s and early 1970s.

With inflation and lower productivity growth translated into
increased production costs, requests to the regulatory agencies for
increased revenues virtually exploded after the late 1960s (as shown
in Table 33). The agencies generally responded by granting less
than the amounts requested, which could be expected, but also
less than the amounts required to maintain investment. Price
changes in the regulated industries, which in 1965–1969 lagged
behind the rest of the economy, were roughly comparable to those
in the unregulated service industries during the 1970s. But the
allowed price increases were less than the realized cost changes,
especially in those industries that use large amounts of fuel (see
Table 34).

Given such regulatory problems, profit margins on sales fell in
the first half of the 1970s to the extent that the public utilities were
generally poor investments for stockholders. Particularly during
the recovery from the recession of 1974–1975, investments in the
regulated industries were less profitable than those in other industries, and far less profitable than they had been in the same industries during the 1960s. Moreover the riskiness of returns on these
investments had increased, given the added uncertainties concern-
ing the ability of these firms to make their dividend payments over
inflationary and low growth periods. Profit rates of return were
low in the early 1970s, from 5.1 percent in the gas utility to 5.5

16. This theme is developed at length in Frank M. Gollop, ''The Sources of
Growth in the U.S. Electric Power Industry'' (paper presented at the Conference
on Productivity Measurement in Regulated Indutries, University of Wisconsin,
1979).

TABLE 33 *Rate Case Proceedings, 1966–1978*[a]

Industry	1966–1969	1970–1973	1974–1978
Electric			
Number of cases	42	78	124
Revenues (millions of dollars)	21	802	2306
Natural gas			
Number of cases	47	64	73
Revenues (millions of dollars)	31	261	651

[a] Average annual number of cases and revenue requests granted.
SOURCES: See Table 24.

TABLE 34   *Prices and Costs in the Regulated Energy Industries, 1969–1980*[a]

Industry	1969–1973		1973–1979		1979–1980	
	Unit prices	Unit costs[b]	Unit prices	Unit costs[b]	Unit prices	Unit costs[b]
Electric	5.7	8.7	11.7	12.7	11.5	12.2
Natural gas	7.9	8.9	18.2	18.9	11.5	11.8
Total regulated	5.1	6.7	8.2	8.5	9.7	10.7
Unregulated services	4.6	4.7	7.9	7.9	9.9	10.2
Total U.S. economy	5.1	5.1	7.5	7.6	9.0	9.9

[a] % average annual rate of change.

[b] See Table 24.

SOURCES: U.S. Department of Labor, Bureau of Labor Statistics, unpublished data (June 1982); *Economic Report of the President* (February 1982), Table B–3; U.S. Department of Labor, Bureau of Labor Statistics, unpublished data (November 1979); *Economic Report of the President* (January 1979).

percent in the electric industry (see Table 30). The more depressed gas investments recovered a little, to the 8 percent range, in the late 1970s. But on the whole the regulated companies were providing stockholder returns which were lower than bondholder interest returns.

Without being able to offer commensurate returns, the regulated companies failed to obtain funds from the capital markets for continued high rates of expansion. After a point, amounts both sought and realized fell off (see Table 35). Investments by the natural gas transmission companies were reduced to levels required to maintain deliveries, while those of the electric companies were falling behind the growth in demand. The reduction in net investment eventually led to reduced rates of production growth by the middle 1970s (see Table 36). Of course these reductions were in keeping with economywide recessionary conditions, first in the early and then in the middle 1970s. Before this period, however, the energy public utility industries had grown at twice the rate of the economy on the whole, while in the 1973–1977 period they did not grow at all, which was certainly below the economywide rate.

Both the regulatory agencies and companies were concerned about these supply-side reactions to inflation and public policy conditions. Efforts were made in the electric power industry to adhere to previous standards of service. To this end, certain policy changes were made, such as adding more to charges for "frills" than for basic service, while at the same time letting up on the obligation of the companies to provide more and wider access to basic service. In the gas industry, existing customers were provided service as long as supplies lasted while new customers were not allowed on the system in many markets. Even with such attempts to contain the erosion of service, the quality of offerings in these industries declined significantly (as shown in Table 37). To be sure, electricity consumers had as much access to service as before, but only because peak demands had been drastically reduced by the economywide recession. On the whole, available capacity relative to expected demands declined; as shown in Table

TABLE 35   *Investment and Capacity Growth in the Regulated Industries, 1969–1981*[a]

Industry	Source	1969–1973	1973 to date	1979–1981
Electric utilities	BEA	7.0	5.9 (1978)	—
Gas transmission	BLS	2.8	2.0 (1974)	—
Total U.S. economy	BEA	3.7	3.2 (1979)	2.9

[a]% average annual rate of change.

SOURCES: U.S. Department of Labor, Bureau of Labor Statistics (BLS), Capital Stock Estimates for Input-Output Industries: Methods and Data, 1979; U.S. Department of Labor, Bureau of Labor Statistics, Office of Economic Growth, unpublished data (April 1979); U.S. Department of Commerce, Bureau of Economic Analysis (BEA).

TABLE 36 *Rates of Output Growth in the Regulated Energy Industries, 1965–1980*[a]

Industry	1965–1969	1969–1973	1973–1979	1979–1980
Electric	7.1	6.3	4.0	2.2
Natural gas	6.5	0.7	−0.7	2.2
Unregulated services	4.0	3.9	2.6	−0.6
Total U.S. economy	3.9	3.4	2.8	−0.2

[a] % average annual rate of change. *Note:* Output growth is measured in terms of real gross national product.

SOURCES: U.S. Department of Labor, Bureau of Labor Statistics, unpublished data (June 1978); *Economic Report of the President* (February 1982), Table B–7; U.S. Department of Labor, Bureau of Labor Statistics, unpublished data (1978); *Economic Report of the President* (January 1979).

TABLE 37 *Service Quality in the Regulated Industries, 1965–1979[a]*

Industry / Index[b]	1965	1969	1973	Latest Year	
Electric					
Expected capability margin	109	110	96	62	(1979)
Outage rate (1969 = 100)	n.a.	100	100[c]	100[c]	(1978)
Natural gas					
Reserve capacity	84	63	52	52	(1977)
Curtailments	100	100	93	76	(1978)

[a]Service quality index, 1958 = 100; n.a. = not available.

[b]Higher index indicates improved service.

[c]Electric outage data do not lend themselves to indexing. In 1969 there were no reported load reductions ("brownouts") and non-weather-related outages were virtually nil. By 1973 load reductions affected approximately 0.1% of all power delivered that year, and blackouts had increased tenfold since 1969. Blackouts rose to three times the 1969 level in 1978, while the proportion of power affected by load reductions continued to rise, to 0.5% of power delivered.

SOURCES: See Table 26.

38, the industry anticipated operating well below the preferred reserve margin of 20 percent during the 1970s.[17]

Customers of gas service had far less access to supply in the 1970s than five to ten years earlier. The regulation-induced shortage of gas production in the Southwest had worked its way through the system to curtailments of industrial and commercial service. The consequent loss of service was highly disruptive, since it made no allowance for efficiency in final fuel use, or for conservation, or for investment and production in energy-using industries.

The various measures of service quality indicate that the regulated companies were no longer providing significant improvements in the volume and quality of service each year. But by 1980 these conditions had been limited only to service reductions for new customers. The occurrence of worsening general price inflation or of more adverse regulatory decisions could have caused curtailments of gas service that would not have been so easily accommodated. Without capacity to expand electricity generation, consumers also could have been faced with the first power disruptions and shortages. Thus established public utility regulatory practices impose substantial costs on the economy, particularly in times of low demand growth and high inflation. Price controls prove to be rigid, and service as a consequence eventually becomes unreliable. While regulatory commissions may, by controls, obtain for all consumers access to the system at low rates in the short run, they do so by compounding problems of decreased productivity growth and increased capital and fuel costs in the long run. Once again regulation in the energy sector has exacerbated conditions of supply stringency through unresponsive price controls.

17. From the 1950s to the mid-1960s electric utilities installed new capacity ahead of expected demand. Then, for reasons explained in the text, their ability to expand service became constrained. Serious power shortages in the 1970s were averted only because exogenous factors forced a reduction in demand growth, which offset the supply curtailments.

TABLE 38 *Capability Margins in the Electric Power Industry, 1958–1980*

Capability margin	1958	1961	1965	1969	1973	1979	1980
Expected[a]	18.7%	26.9%	20.3%	20.5%	17.9%	11.5%	10.7%
Actual	25.9%	31.0%	22.9%	16.6%	20.8%	36.1%	30.8%

[a] "Expected" figure calculated from EEI data (given in thousands of kilowatts) for year t as follows: (actual capability margin for year t minus the predicted capability margin for year $t - 4$, as given in year $t - 4$) divided by (the predicted capability margin for year t, as given in year $t - 4$).

SOURCE: Edison Electric Institute, *Electric Power Survey* (various years).

Prospects for Restoration of Service Quality

The widespread adverse nature of these results has generated some support for reducing the most severely constraining controls. Making changes in regulations, however, has been difficult, because of both short- and long-term effects on established customers. Even a partial lifting of controls could result in extremely large short-term price increases, as has been the case in natural gas. These effects could be offset by long-term gains, but highly visible disruptions would occur immediately and the full benefits of any forthcoming increases in supply would not be realized for many years. Furthermore, partial decontrol of prices and service offerings, in which only some of the regulated markets were freed of controls, could leave the company with requirements to provide nonremunerative service in the regulated markets while not being able to obtain higher than the competitive profits on the decontrolled services.

Even so, the condition of the regulated energy industries that developed in the 1970s has made change imperative. Prices must be able to respond to changes in cost and demand conditions. This requires new procedures that would permit revenue increases sufficient to cover current and near-future cost increases.

The procedure would be to allow any proposed rate increase to go into effect, with later repayment to consumers of any realized "excess" profits. Excess profits would be defined as the difference between realized net profit rates in the period during which the increased revenues were collected and alternative rates of return on investments generally. Such a regulatory practice, comparing the same year's profits across all sectors, would be based more securely on financial data than the present method of comparing past costs and future prices.

While such procedures have not been widely implemented, at least the principle has been accepted. Statute mandates generally require that commissions provide the public utility with an opportunity to earn a rate of return sufficient to maintain the company's financial integrity, attract necessary capital, and compensate investors for risk.[18] To meet this requirement, commissions and agencies made some concessions to the economic conditions of the 1970s by putting in place automatic rate increases resulting from certain quantifiable increases in operating expenses. For one, automatic adjustment of rates to account for fuel cost increases is now permitted in the electric and gas utilities in a large number of states. Attempts have been made to extend the automatic adjustment process to costs other than fuel. The practice has not been widespread, although in a few important cases costs have been indexed to the consumer or producer price index. In New Mexico, for example, the state commission has instituted an indexing plan for the Public Service Company of New Mexico. The results have been encouraging, in that the utility has been reporting both higher profits and smaller rate increases than the national average.[19] More recently, the Michigan Public Service Commission has adopted an indexing system for Consumers Power and Detroit Edison Companies that allows pass-through of nonpower operating costs based entirely on changes in the consumer price index. These provisions, however, would have to be adopted much more widely before the performance of the regulated industries would be significantly improved.[20]

Still another approach has the state commissions consider estimates of future costs as the basis for revenue increases. Since 1977 the New York Public Service Commission has considered estimates of costs for "future test years," even though they have

18. See *Bluefield Water Works & Improvement Co. v. Public Service Commission of the State of West Virginia,* 262 U.S. 79 (1923), pp. 692–93; *Federal Power Commission v. Hope Natural Gas Co.,* 320 U.S. 591 (1944), p. 603 (a regulated utility should be permitted to earn at a rate equal to that experienced by firms in industries characterized by comparable or corresponding risks).

19. Public Service Commission of New Mexico, Case No. 1196 (April 15, 1975). In part these results flow from the higher bond rating the utility has earned because of increased investor certainty over the adequacy of future rate increases. The utility has realized substantial savings in interest payments.

20. Pass-through of costs for some inputs but not others could introduce a bias toward selecting technologies relatively intensive in those inputs for which cost recovery is assured. Provisions for automatic fuel adjustment only, for example, could discourage the shift away from fuel-intensive processes.

necessarily been speculative and subject to substantial errors of forecast.[21] More generally, the state regulatory commissions have been reviewing requests for rate increases in new procedures that have greatly reduced the time required to approve a price change. This has been done by allowing the proposed higher rates to take effect before the decision, subject to repayment of any excess charges after the decision is reached. For example, although electricity case decisions in 1977 took four months longer than in 1971, rate increases took less time to be put into effect.[22]

Most important, the regulatory agencies have been allowing larger increases. This tendency to acquiesce to higher revenue requests has resulted partly from higher estimates of costs, now that historical costs reflect the sharp increases in construction and interest expenses of the early and middle 1970s. But it has also resulted from relaxation of the standards for deciding what is to be included in costs for rate-setting purposes. The new approach has varied from state to state, of course, but many commissions have permitted the inclusion of the costs of construction work in progress in the rate base for rate-making purposes. With substantial construction projects under way at the time of the change, particularly in the electric power industry, this practice has increased the possibility of justifying revenue increases. Also, a number of state commissions have changed their treatment of federal tax savings from accelerated depreciation and the investment tax credit to allow the utilities to retain more of the net cash flow from these provisions. (The coverage of these changes in state regulatory practice is shown in Table 39.)

These changes in regulatory practice for the most part have been in the right direction, but they have not gone far enough to reverse the widespread decline in the service provided by these industries. As a result the outlook remains poor with respect to

21. Michela English, "The Problem of Attracting Capital Faced by Investor-Owned Electric Utilities and Possible Regulatory Solutions," Working Paper Series A, No. 38, Yale University School of Organization and Management (1979), p. 28.

22. Edison Electric Institute, *1978 Annual Electric Power Survey* (1978).

TABLE 39 *Administrative Reforms in Electric Utility Regulation*[a]

Reform[b]	Full use	Partial use	No use
Future test year	19	1	30
Automatic fuel adjustment clause	43	—	7
Construction work in progress (CWIP)	26	8	16
Normalized tax savings	40	6	4

[a]Number of states. *Note*: All tabulations include the District of Columbia and exclude Nebraska, which has no investor-owned electric utilities.

[b]These reforms are explained in the text.

SOURCE: Merrill Lynch, Pierce, Fenner & Smith, Inc., Securities Research Division, "Utility Industry: Quarterly Regulatory Report" (June 1982).

both the quality and the coverage of service. Even with reductions in service coverage and with some rate relief, a shortfall of total capital requirements is likely. This capital shortage will manifest itself in curtailments or reduced quality of service at fixed rates.

Such is the prognosis if the economy continues to operate with regulation much as it now takes place. To the contrary, those industries in which regulation is relaxed would perform better, with fewer shortages or disruptions of service in the 1980s. Even so, great difficulties block those substantial reforms required to produce significant improvements in industry performance. An unfortunate characteristic of regulation in these industries has been that the consequences of current policies are unplanned, untimely, undesirable, and yet resistant to change.

5

◇◇◇◇◇

Energy Policy for the 1980s

A<small>N IMPORTANT LESSON</small> from the energy policy of the last decade was brought home in 1979. During the first quarter of that year, reductions of crude oil from Iran caused worldwide crude supply stringency and price increases. Most buying countries at that time began to use their inventories to add to immediate supplies so as to cushion the shock of the very substantial worldwide crude supply reduction. But instead of reducing inventories the United States took the full impact of the cutback in world shipments in consequent sharp price increases and responded with the established array of price controls and allocation practices. This country subsequently became the only large purchasing nation experiencing significant shortages over the middle part of the year. Thus no substantial progress had been made in dealing with sharp world supply reductions, even though Congress had passed numerous pieces of legislation to increase security and the White House had installed a federal control apparatus second to none to accomplish that result. Worse still, the cause of the shortages in 1979 lay with the response mechanisms of the emergency allocation and pricing systems themselves.

This was not the only lesson of the decade. If it were, then the country's energy problems would have been remedied by the elimination of petroleum products controls carried out by President Reagan early in 1981. It became apparent as well that there are still natural gas and electricity supply problems, and that these are not being dealt with successfully under present policy.

Natural gas had been in a state of serious shortage for a number of years, only to be temporarily in surplus at the end of the decade. Both conditions were the result of regulations that first kept prices too low, and then in the Natural Gas Policy Act allocated supplies to the national market from intrastate sources previously free of controls. As the surplus works off over the early 1980s, and as gas supplies become freer of controls after 1985, substantial price increases are in the offing. These could be so sharp and politically disruptive as to lead to reimposition of controls. There need to be substantial changes in present gas price controls and in the phased decontrol process before 1985 if regulation in the face of these disruptions is not to become permanent.

There are going to be serious and widespread problems with the adequacy of electric power as well. The lack of growth of capacity in the electric power industry in recent years has produced a condition of potential shortage of electricity for consumers in the late 1980s. Furthermore, what electricity will be produced is going to be derived from the wrong mix of fuels. Both result from the present use of the regulatory process of rate-base, rate-of-return regulations by which prices are not allowed to increase commensurate with costs when costs are rising rapidly. The regulatory process has to be changed to allow rapid and flexible adjustment of revenues to changing cost and demand conditions.

How serious are these problems in the aggregate? To date no answer to this question has been made, although there have been urgent and repeated pleadings to the effect that each separate policy malfunction by itself is important. One way of providing an assessment is to compare the current spectrum of fuel use with what reasonably would have been the utilization pattern in the absence of these particular regulations. The difference can then be designated as a cost in terms of the extra payments that had to be made for the misallocation, and the size of that dollar outlay can be used to measure the magnitude of the energy policy problem.

Energy Shares and Costs

In 1970 approximately one-quarter of total energy supplies consisted of coal, hydropower, and nuclear fuels used to produce electricity, another third was natural gas, and the remaining consisted of petroleum products. In 1980, because of the growth of nuclear capacity, electricity accounted for 4 percent more. The decline of natural gas supplies caused that fuel to drop 6 percent. The two together required an increase of 2 percent in the share of petroleum products over the decade. (See the quantities and percentage shares shown in Table 40.)

The overall stability of shares is remarkable. The disparities among fuel prices that developed after the large increases in petroleum prices in the mid-1970s should have led to substantial shifts toward lower priced fuels. The growth in petroleum shares is also quite remarkable—given that gasoline and fuel oil prices increased much more than those for natural gas and the electricity-input fuels.

In fact the fixity of shares has been the result of regulated incapacity to increase the supplies of the less expensive fuels. The lack of capacity of gas field markets under price-ceiling regulations to provide additional supplies was substantial by the early 1970s. As shortages developed, they were resolved as industrial purchasers shifted to residual and heating fuel oils. In the absence of more cheap natural gas, petroleum products have served as substitutes given that there has been no substantial limit on crude oil imports. Demands for petroleum products also increased because rate regulatory policies slowed the rate of conversion of electric power capacity to coal.

The magnitudes of such effects from policy can be seen in the difference between actual market shares in 1980 and those hypothetical shares that would have been realized without any constraints. Estimating hypothetical shares requires the following line of reasoning: upon the initiation of petroleum price increases, without controls, prices of other fuels rise to reestablish the standard price differences due only to transportation costs and fuel

TABLE 40 *Fuel Consumption*[a]

Fuel	1970	1975	1980
Coal	13.75 (20.0)	12.83 (18.2)	15.60 (20.5)
Petroleum[b]	29.78 (43.3)	32.73 (46.3)	34.19 (44.9)
Natural gas	22.35 (32.5)	19.95 (28.2)	20.49 (26.9)
Hydroelectric	2.64 (3.8)	3.22 (4.6)	3.12 (4.1)
Nuclear	0.23 (0.3)	1.90 (2.7)	2.70 (3.5)
	68.76 (100.0)	70.64 (100.0)	76.10 (100.0)

[a]In quadrillion BTUs; figures in parentheses are percent.

[b]Includes natural gas liquids.

SOURCES: 1970—U.S. Bureau of Mines, *Monthly Petroleum Statement*, December 1970, Table 4; 1975 and 1980—DOE / EIA, *Monthly Energy Review*, December 1981, pp. 22–25.

quality. Once price ratios are reestablished, then the trend of market shares established prior to regulation continues to hold.[1] Thus hypothetical market shares can be constructed from multiplying preregulation trend shares by 1973–1980 total fuel consumption.

Actual and hypothetical shares are reflected in the net balance changes in Table 41. The hypothetical shares are derived from historical linear trends of coal / gas / petroleum for the period 1960–1972 as extrapolated for 1973–1980.[2] The net volume differences for gas result from industrial and commercial buyers' moving into petroleum markets when they were forced to curtail their gas consumption by the Federal Power Commission and later by the Federal Energy Regulatory Commission. Gas demands shifted into crude markets increased crude oil demands by almost three quadrillion BTUs, or 1.5 million barrels per day. The implied shifts from coal to petroleum were actually amounts of coal consumption that should have followed from switching to that fuel. The switching did not take place because of reduced electricity capacity growth and because of actual slowdowns in the conversion of plants in operation. In any event, the amounts involved were much smaller, coming to less than one-half quadrillion BTUs. In addition, consumption of crude from foreign sources rather than out of domestic crude production increased because of wellhead price controls in the EPCA. The total shift to crude oil, and thus to imports, probably came to six quadrillion BTUs, or three million barrels per day, by 1980.

1. The assumptions are that as a consequence of the price increases across all fuels, the percentage changes in supply of each fuel are the same. Thus the elasticities of supply have to be constant and identical to those in the earlier period for each fuel over the range of price changes. Also, technology and changes in demands alone dictate shares, not absolute price changes. To the extent that elasticities of supply of coal and gas now exceed that of crude oil, these assumptions imply shares that lead to underestimates of the costs of the various regulatory constraints.

2. Of course the period 1960–1972 was not free of government intervention in the energy industries. No period since World War II has that characteristic. Yet this period, comparable to 1973–1980 in many other respects, saw considerably fewer and less extensive government regulations of energy markets. Thus 1973–1980 can be compared to this earlier, more market-oriented period to estimate the costs of resource misallocation from the energy policies initiated during and after the Arab oil embargo.

TABLE 41 *Policy-Determined Shifts to Petroleum*[a]

Fuel	1975	1980
From natural gas to petroleum	1.04	2.97
From coal to petroleum	−0.38	−0.44
From domestic to imported crude oil	2.96	2.66

[a] In quadrillion BTUs.

SOURCE: For natural gas and coal, the difference between the trend line of 1960–1972 shares and actual shares as shown in Table 40; for crude oil, cf. Table 9.

These departures from the ideal composition of fuel use were costly to consumers, in terms of both expenditures on fuels and security of supply. That gas and coal were cheaper but unavailable was costly. If regulations had been removed so that prices of gas could have risen and demands for coal could have been made evident, then less would have been spent on the total market basket of fuels than actually was spent under controls. The amounts that could have been "saved" can be estimated conservatively by splitting the difference between existing fuel prices and those establishing market equivalents with petroleum, given transportation and processing cost differences. Estimating these "savings" for 1975 and 1980, as in Table 42, from $2 to $16 billion per annum of expenditures could have been avoided. These resource expenditures to pay the bill for imported energy sources would not have had to be paid for more domestic production of crude, gas, or coal in the absence of these policies.[3]

There was more of a shift away from the coal market than shown by the trend of shares, however. The electricity-generating companies had opportunities to switch out of natural gas and residual fuel oils to coal, and these opportunities became increasingly profitable after petroleum products prices tripled in the late 1970s. But substantial capital investments were required to switch old plants to coal, not only for boiler reconstruction but also for stack pollution-control devices required by Environmental Protection Agency regulations. The increased expenditures of capital would in many cases have been paid for out of savings on fuel outlays once the low-priced coal had replaced the high-priced fuel oil. But rate regulation procedures slowed down and reduced investments in such plant changes, even though they would have been

3. At the same time there were substantial risks for all consumers from adding to imports—those risks inherent in adverse economywide reactions to interruptions of imported supply similar to those in 1974 and 1979. By adding three million barrels per day to total imports, the policies of the 1970s reduced rather than increased security of supply. The dollar magnitudes of the cost of these risks cannot be measured adequately to justify an estimate at this time, but the extent of increased insecurity created by these policies was certainly greater at the end of the decade than at any time after the end of the 1974 embargo.

TABLE 42 *Resource Costs of Policy Shifts to Petroleum ($ billions)*

Source	1975	1980
From natural gas to petroleum	0.497	14.101
From coal to petroleum	0.017	0.157
From domestic to imported crude oil	1.393	2.184

SOURCES: Policy-determined shifts to petroleum in Table 41 multiplied by half the difference between alternative fuel prices. These differences are not of the price disparities already in existence before 1973 due to costs of transportation or of pollution and capital requirements.

cost saving as well as conserving of petroleum fuels. This slow-down had effects as shown in Table 43. They imply that crude imports could have been reduced by another 0.8 million barrels per day if operations, rather than being extended in existing plants, were switched to coal-using technologies.[4] As a result, the costs to the economy of energy policy exceeded the $16 billion per annum estimated in 1980 in Table 42. Indeed the cost savings

4. The problems inherent in switching to coal are indicated by the slow transfer of existing plants from other fuels. The accompanying table shows the results for 126 plants, 42 of which were ordered by the DOE to switch to coal. Only half of those so required had completed the transfer by 1982, accounting for one-third of the megawatts of capacity. Of the total 126 plants, 48 had converted or were in process, accounting for 40% of the total capacity. Most of the rest were delayed because of an inability to finance the conversion under existing levels of regulated returns, according to the testimony of corporate representatives. Very few plants, accounting for less than 5% of total capacity, were not converting because of strict environmental restrictions on fuel use.

Electricity Generating Plants Potentially Convertible to Coal

Order issued under	Number of units	Size (Mw)	Converted or in process	Still pending	Conversion delayed because of environmental / financial reasons[c]	Conversion prevented by environmental controls
FUA[a]	25	5,189	13 (2569 Mw)	5 (1225 Mw)	7 (1395 Mw)	—
ESECA[b]	17	2,279	8 (1051 Mw)	4 (761 Mw)	3 (370 Mw)	2 (115 Mw)
No order issued	89	12,963	27 (4779 Mw)	16 (2858 Mw)	35 (4423 Mw)	11 (903 Mw)
Total	131	20,449	48 (8399 Mw)	25 (4844 Mw)	45 (6188 Mw)	13 (1018 Mw)

[a]Powerplant and Industrial Fuel Use Act, PL 95–620, 1978–79, 92 U.S. Statutes at Large 3289.

[b]Energy Supply and Environmental Coordination Act of 1974, PL 93–319, 1974, 88 U.S. Statutes at Large 246.

[c]Utilities with regulated rates of return cannot raise the capital necessary to finance required emission-control devices. In the absence of rate ceilings, the companies could finance conversion by passing the costs along to the consumers.

SOURCE: Telephone calls based on the list of *Powerplants Capable of Being Converted to Coal*, ICF, August 29, 1979. Units which came on line before 1940 or which are smaller than 25 Mw were excluded as per DOE procedure. Also excluded are units identified as not feasible conversion candidates by the utility in question.

TABLE 43 *Electric Powerplant Fuel Switching*[a]

Categories of conversions covered by ESECA[b] and FUA[c]	Potential conversions (Mw capacity)	Realized conversions (Mw capacity)	Fuel use in unrealized conversions (quadrillion BTUs)
1. Plants for which conversion is feasible:			
(a) Plants with SO_2 emissions limitations greater than 1.2 lbs SO_2 per MM BTU	16,222	10,985	0.31
(b) Plants with SO_2 emissions limitations less than 1.2 lbs SO_2 per MM BTU	3,325	74	0.19
2. Plants for which conversion is technically difficult:			
(a) Plants with SO_2 emissions limitations greater than 1.2 lbs SO_2 per MM BTU	4,738	131	0.28
(b) Plants with SO_2 emissions limitations less than 1.2 lbs SO_2 per MM BTU	661	0	0.04
3. Total of all categories	24,946	11,190	0.82

TABLE 43 (Continued)

[a]*Note:* Electric utilities covered by the Energy Supply and Environmental Coordination Act of 1974 and the Powerplant and Industrial Fuel Use Act of 1978 were categorized by ICF, Inc., according to the technical difficulty involved in conversion to coal. These plants, listed by megawatts of capacity, were then divided into two groups for unrealized and realized conversions. The megawatts of capacity involved in unrealized conversions were translated into quadrillion BTUs of fuel by multiplying (1) the number of kilowatt-hours of output per year associated with the capacity, times (2) the number of BTUs embodied in a kilowatt-hour of output, where:

$$(1) \ kWh/yr = (Mw \times 1000) \times 8760 \times 0.65$$

$$ \begin{array}{ccc} \text{kilowatts of} & \text{no. of hours} & \text{load} \\ \text{capacity} & \text{per year} & \text{factor} \end{array}$$

$$(2) \ BTU/kWh = 10{,}500$$

For every 1000 megawatts of capacity then, the amount of fuel used over the course of a year is the product of (1) and (2) which is equal to 0.059 quadrillion BTUs. The 1000 megawatts of capacity involved in unrealized conversion has been multiplied by 0.0598 and the product has been designated as the fuel use associated with unrealized conversions under the ESECA and FUA.

[b]Energy Supply and Environmental Coordination Act.

[c]Powerplant and Industrial Fuel Use Act.

SOURCES: DOE, Economic Regulatory Administration memoranda: "Proposed Prohibition Orders—Fuel Use Act" and "Summary Sheet of ESECA Utility Orders," with realized conversions noted by Steve Frank, Chief, Prohibition Order Section, Economic Regulatory Administration; DOE, Economic Regulatory Administration, *Fuels Conversion Program Powerplant Profiles*, January 1981; DOE/EIA, *Monthly Energy Review*.

foregone was probably of a magnitude that caused total costs of energy policy to approach $20 billion in the late 1970s.

Production Shares and Levels in the 1980s

The new decade is expected to bring forth both higher levels of consumption and much more switching to less costly and more secure fuels. Consumption levels are expected to increase by twelve quadrillion BTUs before 1990. The increase is to come from expanded coal and nuclear fuel utilization in the production of electric power. Furthermore, petroleum and natural gas utilization are expected to decline by almost three quadrillion BTUs, while coal and nuclear fuels are to increase by fourteen quadrillion BTUs (as can be seen from comparing the forecasts in Table 44 with the estimates of 1980 fuel use in Table 40).

The shift to coal, if realized, would be a remarkable change in fuel-utilization patterns, requiring radical changes in energy policy and market conditions. One incentive is the expected change in prices of other fuels. Petroleum products prices are forecast to increase by more than 50 percent over the decade in current dollars.[5] The conservation effects of such another large price increase would be expected to reduce consumption and thereby imports by roughly two quadrillion BTUs. Natural gas prices are expected to increase, at least to the extent implied by the Natural Gas Policy Act, in a sequence of steps through 1987. The steps would bring field prices of gas in line roughly 90 percent of the level of crude oil prices, so that both were expensive relative to coal. The relative cheapness of coal, which is expected to be priced at present levels, could well lead to substantial switching of fuels in existing plants and to the dedication of all new electric generation capacity to this fuel.

Other sources could add marginally to domestic energy supply during this decade. The existing nuclear fission technology can be expected to be utilized to add approximately five quadrillion BTUs

5. DOE / EIA, *Annual Report to Congress 1981*, vol. 3, February 1982.

TABLE 44 *Forecasts of 1990 United States Energy Supply Mix*

	Petroleum (%)	Natural gas (%)	Nuclear (%)	Coal (%)	Total energy consumption (quadrillion BTUs)
Department of Energy	35.4	19.6	9.2	31.7	87.0
Data Resources, Inc.	35.2	22.9	8.3	28.4	87.6
Bankers Trust	33.7	22.3	9.3	28.3	91.1
DOE Policy Group	34.8	22.9	8.2	27.1	90.5
Exxon Corporation	39.6	20.4	8.0	24.0	87.2

SOURCES: DOE / EIA, *Annual Report to Congress 1980*, 3:107; Data Resources, Inc., *Energy Review*, Autumn 1980; Bankers Trust Co., *U.S. Energy and Capital Forecast 1980–90*, Summer 1980; DOE, Policy and Evaluation, *Reducing U.S. Oil Vulnerability*, November 1980; Exxon Co. USA, *Energy Outlooks 1980–2000*, December 1980.

to capacity, assuming only that plants now under construction are completed.[6] The production of fuels from heavy crude oils, and of manufactured gas from coal, could add up to one quadrillion BTUs but only under the most favorable of results in the development of new technology for cost containment. Only these two of the new technologies are likely to develop without substantial government subsidy, and to produce fuels at costs roughly comparable to crude oil at $35.00 per barrel or to gas at $5.00 per quadrillion BTUs.[7]

Even so, the quantity and mix of fuels still depends critically

6. The table below indicates the forecasts and the status quo in reactor energy production as of 1980:

Forecasted Increases in Nuclear Energy Production, 1980–1990

1980 actual level	EIA	DRI	Bankers Trust	Policy & Evaluation	Exxon
2.7 quadrillion BTUs	196%	170%	215%	174%	159%

These percentages have been calculated by subtracting the 1980 level production in quadrillion BTUs (quads) from the forecast 1990 level in quads, then dividing by the 1980 level in quads for each source. The capacity to be added and its production can be determined by adding up the capacity of new plants expected to be on line in the late 1980s. Total megawatt capacity of nuclear powerplants currently in the operating license stage with starting dates through 1990 is 72,032 megawatts. Assuming that

$$(72{,}032 \times 1000) \times .75 \times 8760 = 4.97 \text{ quads/yr.}$$
$$\text{(kilowatts)} \quad \text{(load)} \quad \text{(hours)}$$

4.97 additional quads by 1990 translates into a total level of 7.67 which represents an increase of 184% between 1980 and 1990. The average of the five forecast percentage increases above is 183%.

7. Optimistic forecasts of the Department of Energy add another quadrillion BTUs to supply from oil shale production from presently active projects (capable of 200,000 barrels per day of equivalent crude oil production) and now suspended projects (such as Union Ridge and Colony, also capable of producing 200,000 barrels per day if in operation). (Cf. Department of Energy, *Reducing U.S. Oil Vulnerability: Energy Policy for the 1980s,* November 10, 1980. Cf. also Report by the Subcommittee on Synthetic Fuels of the Committee on the Budget, United States Senate, September 27, 1979.) But these would require substantial federal subsidies, not now expected to be available, and they have long lead times before full operation, so that any such source of a quadrillion BTUs has to be discounted.

on energy policy. The admonition in Chapter 1 to hold back from invoking more energy policy is not enough. There have to be substantial reductions in present policy for the forecast total volume to become available on schedule, and for the fundamental shift to coal to take place. Deregulation of natural gas prices has to be completed for conservation efforts to be fully realized. Profits taxation of crude oil has to be eliminated to add to domestic supply. Most important, substantial regulatory reform in electricity production and distribution has to be accomplished to foster the purchase of coal-burning equipment rather than the maintenance of facilities using other fuels.

The first key to achieving the correct energy consumption level is the elimination of controls over natural gas prices and production. The Natural Gas Policy Act of 1978 was based on the premise that there inevitably would be gas shortages from regulation, and that any new policy should be directed to methods for further regulation to decide which industrial consumers would have to absorb these shortages. Phased deregulation set new gas prices at the wellhead in a sequence that increased to world market crude price levels, while old or already-flowing gas prices were kept down to half or less of these levels. New and old gas prices were to be averaged to produce a uniform price level for home consumers below that for heating fuel, and for industrial consumers at equal to that for industrial fuel oil prices in the early and middle 1980s. Shortages went to the industrial consumers not allowed to pay higher prices than for petroleum products, or not allowed to switch to gas from other fuels. But in laying out this price sequence, the NGPA failed to anticipate the actual crude oil price increases that shocked crude markets in 1979 and 1980. The result to date has been a failure to bring industrial gas and fuel oil prices into line, thereby creating additional demands for gas.

Moreover, as disparities between old and new gas prices widened with the higher oil prices, the demands of different pipelines for new gas have been distorted to widely varying degrees. Those pipelines with substantial price-controlled old gas have been able to bid more for new gas, since their higher new gas prices are rolled into more low-priced old gas in the final-product pricing schedules. They continue to obtain the largest proportion of any additional gas brought onto the national market, regardless of whether their resale demands are most extensive.

The policy alternatives come down either to decontrol of old gas prices, or to control completely both old and new prices. Total decontrol eliminates the advantage of the established pipelines in the prices they pay for old, flowing gas supplies. At the same time it provides equal access to all supplies, with the successful bidder achieving the purchase based on the intensity of final demands in wholesale and retail energy markets. The alternative of total regulation also has its advantages—prices would be kept at prevailing or slowly accelerating levels for most home consumers, and no pipeline would gain an advantage in supply from being able to outbid others in the market for additional reserves due to having more old gas at low regulated prices. But shortages would begin to appear as additional reserves were smaller each year. Just as in the early 1970s, exploratory activity would wind down in favor of further work abroad in world crude markets. The quantities of gas available for production and distribution in the United States would fall, probably as early as in the middle 1980s. Consumers protected against price increases would once again be removed from the opportunity to obtain natural gas supplies, and would have to purchase additional imports of foreign crude for heating and process fuel.

The decontrol policy is the only realistic alternative for achieving the forecast volume and mix of fuels in 1990. If the costs of the present energy mix are to be substantially reduced, and crude oil imports eliminated in favor of other fuels, natural gas has to be released from the controls in effect for the last twenty-eight years. To prevent the disparities that give pipelines with old reserves the opportunity to outbid others with new reserves, all price controls should be eliminated.

The first step in achieving these reforms would be to increase prices on all old, flowing gas to levels roughly comparable to those on new gas as of the early 1980s. This can be done now without a substantial price "spike," given present low levels of gas demands resulting from the recession. Any such immediate price increases for flowing sections 104–106 categories of gas would only increase the average price by the same amount. Such a limited current price increase would lead to some increase in production and to important reductions in quantities demanded that would be sufficient to eliminate the deliverability shortage likely otherwise to occur in the mid-1980s. There need be no price "spike" in 1985 if this policy variation is put in place by the FERC in 1982.

The first round of policy effects is clear. These higher prices from the elimination of vintaging would raise average prices for all gas sold to the pipelines. The higher price level would cause demand reductions in the range of 3–4 percent the first year.[8] This would occur just at the time the economy goes into recovery, and would work to hold back the growth of excess demand. Further market price increase, of an additional 17.7 percent in 1983, −2.2 percent in 1984, and 7.6 percent in 1985, would have similar demand-constraining effects (as shown in Table 45).

With the addition of some limited supply response from these early price increases as well, then the 1985 NGPA "price spike" would be avoided. The shock effects would be largely eliminated by decontrolling earlier when demand growth is not present. At the same time advantages of an earlier beginning on national allocation of gas among regions are realized. These results are illustrated in Table 45.

That the alternative policy of immediate price increases cuts

8. The revised version of the MacAvoy-Pindyck Demand Model has been used to estimate overall price elasticities for demand in the 1975–1981 period. The short-term elasticities of residential-commercial and industrial demand are estimated at −0.11 and −0.13, respectively. Weighting these elasticities by their contributions to demand gives us an overall elasticity of about −0.12. Thus an increase in prices from $1.81 to $2.26 per 1000 cubic feet from the NGPA as is to higher sections 104–106 prices would, *ceteris paribus,* reduce demand by about 3.2%. Of course, *mutatis mutandis,* these results do not take into account general equilibrium effects.

TABLE 45 *Forecasts of Price and Quantity Effects from Raising Natural Gas Prices Immediately*

Year	Average domestic price[a]	% change	Marketed production[b]	Demand for marketed production[b]
1981	2.32		18.76	18.76
1982	2.61	12.5	19.09	17.65
1983	3.07	17.7	19.54	17.73
1984	3.01	−2.2	19.83	18.40
1985	3.23	7.6	19.99	19.12
1986	3.54	9.5	19.76	19.76
1987	4.27	20.4	20.01	20.01

[a]In 1981 dollars per 1000 cubic feet.

[b]In trillions of cubic feet.

SOURCE: As described in Table 19.

through the price "spike" in 1985 created by the Natural Gas Policy Act is critical.[9] Prevention of disruptive effects from a 1985 gas price "spike" is a matter of general prudence in economic policy. To be sure, this is not costless—the economy accepts a current, limited price increase to prevent an uncertain but potentially quite large price "spike" in the future. Flowing gas prices on sections 104 and 106 categories should be increased now to section 103 levels to guarantee the smooth operation of market dynamics in 1985 and 1986. This step will eliminate the need for much more complicated and costly regulation thereafter.

The second key reform requires the removal of the indirect regulations on crude oil produced within the United States. These indirect controls are not price ceilings as invoked in the middle 1970s, but rather windfall profits taxes on the difference between the old price ceilings and present market prices. Such taxes have any number of effects, from shifting oil exploration from domestic to foreign operations, to cutting back on investment in all types of domestic refining and marketing. Unless they are removed there will be a higher level of crude imports by as much as a million barrels per day through the 1983–1988 period, which would per-

9. This diagram shows the natural gas price forecasts for the status quo case where prices are deregulated in 1985 in accordance with the NGPA, and the adjusted price case where sections 104, 106, and 109 prices are raised now. Prices are in 1980 dollars.

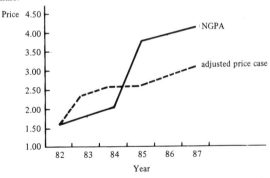

Average Pipeline Acquisition Cost of Domestic Natural Gas for the NGPA and the Alternative Pricing Case

petuate an excessive expenditure.[10] Table 46 shows estimates of the reduction in domestic production consequent from the tax. If the imports substituted for this lost production cost $5.00 more per barrel to purchase from abroad, then the excessive expenditure could approach $2 billion per annum. The removal of the windfall profits tax would eliminate these substantial costs to the economy. To be sure, federal revenues would be reduced by a far greater amount, since the taxes apply to established as well as to additional sources of crude supply. But these taxes can be collected in other ways without having an adverse effect on the domestic supply of liquid fuels.

The third key reform is to change regulations that now prevent the expansion of coal utilization in the production of electricity. Public utility rate regulation of the power industry has had much the same effects as ceiling prices on natural gas, except that the shortages of power are in the future rather than the past. And reform is a much more complicated political process. The major part of the practice of rate regulation has been carried out by state

10. The tax operates to have the same effect on supply and demand as the wellhead price controls of the 1970s. This can be illustrated by the following diagram.

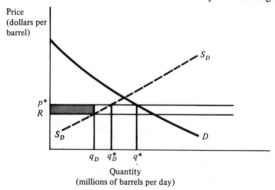

Under price controls, at regulated price R set below world crude price levels, domestic production falls from q_D^* to q_D. The difference is absorbed in increased imports, until market demand at world price p^* is satisfied at q^*. With a windfall tax, the shaded area is paid over in taxes by domestic producers of q_D selling at world prices p^*. The result is the same, as net price falls to R and output is cut back to q_D.

TABLE 46 *Domestic Production of Crude Oil in the 1980s*

	Without windfall profits tax (% annual increase)	With tax (% annual increase)	Difference (millions of barrels / day)
1982	−2.03	0.16	1.018
1983	−1.37	0.82	.742
1984	0.40	0.55	.726
1985	1.25	−0.10	.899
1986	1.04	−0.44	1.088
1987	0.36	−0.30	1.171
1988	0.05	0.06	1.170

SOURCE: "With tax"—Average wellhead price of $11.94 (1972 dollars) for 1980 is forced for 1980–1988 in the Ealy-MacAvoy Model described in the tables for Chapter 2; under "without windfall profits tax"—Ealy-MacAvoy Model simulations at average wellhead prices of $20.04 for 1981, proceeding to $21.99 in 1988 (as shown in Table 4-3 of P. W. MacAvoy, *Crude Oil Prices: As Determined by OPEC and Market Fundamentals* [Cambridge, Mass.: Ballinger, 1982], for an open market for crude oil at world price levels).

agencies, each independently of the others, and only a half dozen of these agencies have the technical facility to make complicated reforms. Any changes would have to follow from new rate case decisions by commissions in the leading states, and such changes would be slow in coming.

At present, substantial capacity shortages are forecast for the late 1980s and early 1990s. The ability to expand capacity has become quite limited as regulation has become more stringent in recent years; even so, there could still be sufficient capacity to meet expected consumer demands until then. But in holding allowed rates of return on equity to less than the cost of capital, the regulatory commissions have not only incurred the risk of shortages but have also slowed down the process of switching presently operating plants to coal-burning facilities. The continuation of low earnings makes the consensus forecast of an increase of 50 percent in coal-burning capacity highly unlikely.

The limits on electricity price increases during inflation have to be set by some method other than rate base regulation. While costs and prices of other services are increasing, electricity prices have to be allowed to increase before regulatory reviews based on past costs are completed and already-dated new prices go into effect. One such change would be to allow rate increases to go into effect as soon as requested in all cases. This would make certain that prices increase commensurate with rising materials and capital costs. If the announced increases turned out in the first year to be excessive, however, then a retrospective review of costs and rates by the commission would find that excess profits had been made. The excess would be subject to repayment to consumers, either in current period rate reductions or in returns of overcharges. Such a policy reform would eliminate regulatory lag and underallowances of the commissions of proposed rate increases. If this were done, then the reallocation of fuel purchases to less costly and more secure coal supplies could be expected to follow as a matter of course.

The urgency of this last key reform can be seen from the slowdown in plant changeovers to coal utilization. The outlook for achieving targets on coal conversion and expansion can be surmised from a very simple set of calculations. From Tables 3 and 45, it can be determined that the forecast growth in coal share implies a necessary increase of approximately 10.0 quadrillion BTUs (quads) in the use of coal. Of that, 2.3 quads would likely come from expansion of industrial use of this fuel.[11] The remaining 7.7 quads has to be based on expansion of coal-using generating capacity in the power industry. But at the present time only 51,700 Mw of capacity are under construction, to be available to use only 3.3 quads of coal per annum. Retirements of 9,900 Mw of capacity in plants more than forty years old would reduce 1990 consumption by 0.6 quads. A further 48,700 Mw have been placed on order,[12] and if every order were confirmed and then completed on schedule, another 3.1 quads of coal consumption would be realized. Yet if half of those plant orders are subject to delay or are cancelled for financial reasons, but still the oldest plants are by necessity retired, then only 2.5 quads would be added to consumption and the total additions would be limited to 4.8 quads from electric power expansion. Normal regulatory conditions halve the volume of energy consumption that is shifted to coal.

The important steps to be taken are in the direction of reducing or eliminating the mistaken and outmoded policy initiatives of the 1970s. There is beyond that, however, a fourth new policy that merits consideration—a tariff on crude oil imports. The case for a tariff is strong on both economic and national security grounds. Markets for crude oil and petroleum products, when faced with a tariff on the marginal sources of supply, end up with a price level higher by the amount of the tariff. This higher price level would reduce product demands and thereby reduce imports.[13] With lower

11. DOE / EIA, *Annual Report to Congress, 1981*, 3:156.

12. National Electric Reliability Council, *Electric Power Supply and Demand, 1981–1990*.

13. The case for a tariff can be illustrated with a diagram as follows. World price is at p^*, and domestic consumption equal to q^* from domestic supply q_D^* and

levels of imports the country would choose to purchase less from those foreign suppliers more likely to embargo shipments to the United States for political or ideological reasons. Even in the absence of an import-control policy geared to national security, private buyers would avoid those producing countries prone to embargoes if they could.

By varying the tariff, this country could also avoid some of the sharp price increases in imported crude that cause federal monetary and fiscal authorities to "ease" (read "monetize") reduced demands for energy and other goods and services. The gains from price and income stability should make us willing to pay a tariff per barrel slightly less than the expected costs per barrel of the supply interruptions avoided. Assuming that the adverse effects of any possible future disruption in one year of the next five would involve another permanent 100 percent crude oil price increase, then any tariff of up to a 20 percent price increase can be justified. Thus a tariff of $10.00 per barrel can be justified if the receipts are recycled to consumers in reduced income taxes.

Such a policy would increase consumer expenditures on energy by up to $50 billion each year. Approximately one-third of that amount would be paid by individuals and corporations as tariffs.

---

imports $(q^* - q_D^*)$. The tariff is passed on to consumers by importers as $p^* + t$, reducing demand from q^* to q and increasing domestic supply to q_D. The amount of tariff payments is shown by the shaded area in the diagram.

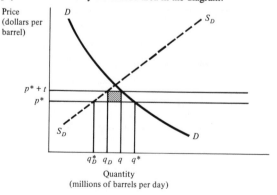

The remains would accrue to domestic crude oil suppliers as profits from increased prices for their domestic (nontariffed) production, but up to half of that amount would again accrue to governments in severance and corporate income taxes. At the same time consumers should get back the government's two-thirds, or $30 billion, in income tax reductions. The higher price for petroleum products consequent upon the tariff should bring about substantially greater conservation, reducing imports by approximately one million barrels per day by 1987–1988 (see Table 47). The higher prices received by domestic producers should provide strong further incentives to increased domestic exploration and development, so as to add approximately one-half to two-thirds of a million barrels per day to domestic supplies (as in Table 47).

These tariff-induced conservation and domestic production effects should keep imports down to less than four million barrels per day in the late 1980s. At that level, given further development of supplies from non-Mideast sources, the United States need not take more than one million barrels per day from any one source. Given the greater reliability of those sources from which we would purchase, this country could hold inventories against any disruption from any one source without excessive expenditures on inventory holding costs.

Three key policy reductions and one key initiative should result in reduced shares for petroleum and natural gas and an increased share for coal of total fuel use in the late 1980s. At the same time the rate of growth of total consumption should be less than half the rate of the early 1970s. Restrained growth and a tariff should substantially reduce imports. This would be without any technical fix and a consequence of the operation of open and uncontrolled markets at present price levels.

Such an outlook is encouraging, but only as long as the four required policy changes are made. As a strategy, they come to eliminating the regulation of energy. The energy policy goals of the 1970s were most often contradictory and incapable of being achieved simultaneously. Limited success was attained in restricting price increases for consumers, but only at the cost of reduced

TABLE 47   *The Effects of an Import Tariff of $10 / Barrel*

	Demand decrease[a]	Domestic supply increase[a]	Tariff payments to treasury[b]	Payments of profits taxes[b]
1982	.226	.820	$45.03	$38.030
1983	.421	.802	43.68	37.253
1984	.601	.637	42.23	38.534
1985	.770	.480	40.23	39.955
1986	.915	.451	37.74	40.000
1987	1.034	.513	35.61	38.767
1988	1.129	.567	34.24	37.673

[a]Millions of barrels per day.

[b]Millions of dollars per day.

SOURCE: Ealy-MacAvoy Model simulations at average wellhead prices of $20.43 for 1982, proceeding to $21.99 for 1988 (as shown in Table 4–3 of Paul W. MacAvoy, *Crude Oil Prices: As Determined by OPEC and Market Fundamentals* [Cambridge, Mass.: Ballinger, 1982]), for an open market for crude oil; tariff payments are the product of $10 / barrel times the amount of imports; payments of profit taxes are the product of tariff price difference, domestic supply, and an approximate tax rate of 40%.

supplies or declines in service quality. Allocation schemes merely created the shortages they were designed to prevent. Overall, the policies worsened U.S. vulnerability to embargoes, increased energy demands, and discouraged substitution of less expensive, more secure fuels. Prices were not stabilized, supplies were less available, and income-distribution goals were left unmet. Overall, the technical fix policies worsened emerging conditions of supply stringency.

The elimination of gas, oil, and electricity price controls would place the final epitaph on the technical fix. In the late 1970s it was destructive, and it could only be more so in the middle and late 1980s. The time and opportunity are present for removing the cause for using too much of the wrong fuels. The mistaken and arrogant energy control policies of the 1970s should be eliminated once and for all.

found in that region, and (3) the amount remaining to be found. Statistical regression equations are developed for each region based on these factors, and the level of new reserves is forecast for future years.

The production of crude oil is based on the size of stocks of both old and newly discovered reserves and the operating limits on the rate of production from those reserves. In addition to these physical factors, the primary market factor is the price: if the price of crude oil increases, then its quantity should increase as well. These relationships are summarized in five supply functions, one for each region, in which production in logarithms is determined by a log-linear equation inclusive of each of these variables.

Crude oil demand is dependent on economic activity, the stock of oil-using equipment, and the prices of both crude and petroleum products. Rising income levels are expected to increase demand, and rising prices are expected to reduce demand, as consumers substitute cheaper alternatives or consume their inventories. The model divides demand into three sectors, based on different histories. The United States as one sector maintained price controls that kept prices above world levels during the late 1960s, but below world levels during the early and middle 1970s. The "developed world" as a second sector includes most of Western Europe and Japan; these countries have historically responded to changes in world crude prices without imposing controls, and with substantial additional sales taxes. The third sector consists of "less developed countries" (LDCs) with relatively small stocks of energy-using equipment but rapidly increasing demands based on a high rate of installation of new equipment.

The supply and demand equations are further specified by values for the price elasticities of supply and demand, the elasticity of demand, and the elasticities of the adjustment to this period's desired level of supply and demand from last period's. These values have been estimated by three different methods. First, statistical methods were used on the data from the pre-1972 period. But the results were spurious, because of a relatively small number of observations. Second, elasticity estimates were excerpted from the research literature. However, these values varied greatly from source to source. The third method was the one actually used, i.e., stipulating the elasticity values, based on the two previous methods, and using them to replicate actual crude market price and production behavior of the 1970s. Those values best able to simulate actual behavior were chosen for use in the model.

TABLE A.1 *Base Case Assumptions*

	United States	LDCs	West
Short-run price elasticity of demand	−0.040	−0.040	−0.040
Short-run income elasticity of demand ten-year adjustment period	0.100	0.100	0.100

	U.S.	OPEC-1	OPEC-2	OPEC-3	World
Short-run price elasticity of supply two-year adjustment period	0.200	0.200	0.200	0.200	0.200
Stock coefficients	1.000	1.000	1.000	1.000	1.000

SOURCE: Paul W. MacAvoy, *Crude Oil Prices: As Determined by OPEC and Market Fundamentals* (Cambridge, Mass.: Ballinger, 1982), p. 44.

Table A.1 details the demand and supply elasticities used in the "base case" of the model.

In order to analyze the effectiveness of the OPEC cartel, the Ealy-MacAvoy Market Model has been used to simulate conditions in the 1970s without OPEC. The results indicate that supply-demand equilibrium would have resulted in higher demand but lower supply increases for the late 1970s so that prices would have risen as shown in Table A.2. The sequence results in a simulated price level in 1979 of $11.11 per barrel, only $.37 per barrel less than the actual price level in the market that year. The simulated price for 1980 would not have been as high as the new market price level, with a $5-per-barrel difference in that year. It is also found that the simulated free-market production rate was substantially more in the late 1970s than actual market production.

In order to forecast prices and quantities for the 1980s, the Ealy-MacAvoy OPEC-Restricted Model is used to incorporate the actual amount of crude oil produced by OPEC in 1980. An open market is then put into operation in 1981, with production rates of the regions OPEC-1 and OPEC-3 assumed to vary with prices according to their supply elasticities, just as in non-OPEC countries. OPEC-2 is held constant at 1980 production rates, on the assumption that Iran and Iraq would continue to hold at 1980 levels partially because of the poor operating condition of their wells and pipelines. With only small increases in OPEC-1 and OPEC-3 production, total supply is much the same from year to year. This results in a constant price level through 1986, and only a 5 percent increase to $22 per barrel in 1988 (see Table A.3).

TABLE A.2 *Supply-Demand Market Price Report*

Year	Change in real world oil prices (%)	Real world oil price (1972 $)	Actual real oil price (1972 $)
1972		2.64	2.64
1973	−10.85	2.35	3.09
1974	135.50	5.54	9.72
1975	−4.08	5.32	9.21
1976	35.36	7.20	9.39
1977	−0.86	7.13	9.53
1978	16.84	8.34	8.95
1979	33.25	11.11	11.48
1980	38.03	15.33	20.46

SOURCE: Paul W. MacAvoy, *Crude Oil Prices: As Determined by OPEC and Market Fundamentals* (Cambridge, Mass.: Ballinger, 1982), pp. 40, 44.

TABLE A.3 *All-OPEC Restricted Model Price Report*

Year	Change in real world oil prices (%)	Real world oil price (1972 $)
1981		20.04
1982	1.96	20.43
1983	0.35	20.51
1984	−0.87	20.33
1985	−0.86	20.15
1986	1.19	20.39
1987	3.24	21.05
1988	4.47	21.99

SOURCE: Paul W. MacAvoy, *Crude Oil Prices: As Determined by OPEC and Market Fundamentals* (Cambridge, Mass.: Ballinger, 1982), p. 68.

Efficiency Losses Due to Distortions in Fuel Market Shares

T HE OBJECT of the following calculations was to determine the efficiency loss resulting from regulation of fuel markets for each year of the period 1973–1980. The analysis is confined to petroleum, natural gas, and coal markets, and residential / commercial and industrial sectors. Because of its low level of coal consumption, the residential / commercial sector was excluded from the study of the coal market.

The loss due to energy regulation was calculated for each year in three steps. First, the distortion in the quantity of each fuel consumed because of the presence of regulation was determined. Second, the change in price of each fuel caused by regulation was found. Finally, the changes in quantities were mutiplied by the changes in prices for all fuels and sectors. These were then summed for each year to give the total value of the loss caused by fuel market regulation.

In determining the difference in quantitites of each fuel consumed by each sector because of regulation, the long-term market shares were first calculated. These were assumed to be free of regulatory effects. To obtain shares, the amount of each fuel used by each sector was divided by the total amount of all energy used by that sector—all in quadrillion BTUs. Table B.1 lists these market shares for 1960–1972.

Long-term percentage shares were determined by fitting trend lines to shares for each fuel and sector for 1960–1972, using the method of ordinary least squares. These regressions were as follows:

TABLE B.1   *Percentage Market Shares*

Year	Residential / commercial natural gas (%)	Industrial Natural gas (%)	Industrial Coal (%)
1960	38.3	37.4	27.0
1961	39.4	38.7	25.9
1962	40.6	39.1	25.3
1963	41.9	39.3	25.3
1964	44.0	38.9	25.5
1965	43.4	39.0	25.8
1966	44.9	39.6	25.2
1967	46.7	40.9	24.0
1968	47.1	42.3	22.7
1969	48.3	43.8	21.4
1970	48.9	44.5	21.1
1971	49.7	46.8	18.2
1972	50.1	45.6	17.8

SOURCE: DOE / EIA, *Annual Report to Congress, 1980*, 2:9, 107, and 129.

1. $RCNG = 37.8 + 1.012T;$ $R^2 = .98$
              $(.043)$

2. $ING = 36.1 + .734T;$ $R^2 = .88$
              $(.081)$

3. $IC = 28.5 - .712T;$ $R^2 = .85$
              $(.894)$

where $RCNG$ = residential / commercial sector consumption of natural gas; ING = industrial sector consumption of natural gas; IC = industrial sector consumption of coal; and T = trend. Predicted market shares were then obtained for 1973–1980 by inserting trend values into these regressions. They are shown in Table B.2.

Last, the actual quantity of each fuel used by each sector was subtracted from the predicted quantity of each fuel (as converted from the market shares in Table B.2) used by each sector for 1973–1980, giving the difference in the quantity consumed of each fuel each year because of the presence of regulation in the 1970s.

The second step in finding the efficiency loss due to regulation involves calculation of the changes in the prices of natural gas and coal relative to petroleum in each year, 1973–1980. The price change for natural gas (or coal) was found through the formula below:

$$\Delta P_{G,t} = P_{0,t} - [P_{G,t} + (\bar{P}_0 - \bar{P}_G)]$$

where $\Delta P_{G,t}$ = the change in the price of natural gas (or coal) due to regulation in year t; $P_{0,t}$ = the price of domestic crude oil at the wellhead in year t; $P_{G,t}$ = the price of natural gas (or coal) in year t; $\bar{P}_0$ = the average price of domestic crude oil at the wellhead for the 1960s; and $\bar{P}_G$ = the average price of natural gas (or coal) for the 1960s. (All prices are in current dollars per quadrillion BTUs.)

The average price of natural gas (or coal) in the 1960s was subtracted from the average price of oil during the 1960s. Then the price of natural gas (or coal) for each year of the period 1973–1980 was added. This latter sum was subtracted from the oil price for each year, 1973–1980—giving the difference in the price of natural gas (or coal) relative to the price of petroleum caused by regulation. (Table B.3 lists the fuel prices for 1960–1980 and Table B.4 lists the actual changes in prices calculated by sector and fuel.)

The final step in calculating the efficiency loss due to regulation

TABLE B.2 *Predicted Market Shares*

Year	Residential / commercial natural gas (%)	Industrial Natural gas (%)	Industrial Coal (%)
1973	52.0	46.4	18.5
1974	53.0	47.1	17.8
1975	54.0	47.8	17.1
1976	55.0	48.6	16.4
1977	56.0	49.3	15.6
1978	57.0	50.0	14.9
1979	58.0	50.8	14.2
1980	59.0	51.5	13.5

SOURCE: Figures generated from a line fitted by ordinary least squares using percentage market shares in Table B.1.

is multiplication of the changes in quantities and prices for natural gas and coal in the residential / commercial and industrial sectors. These figures are presented in Table B.4, giving the efficiency losses by fuel and sector for each year, 1973–1980.

TABLE B.3 *Fuel Prices, 1960–1980*[a]

Year	Petroleum[b]	Natural gas[c]	Coal[a]
1960	489,600,000	140,000,000	206,360,000
1961	491,300,000	151,000,000	201,520,000
1962	493,000,000	155,000,000	197,120,000
1963	491,300,000	158,000,000	193,160,000
1964	489,600,000	154,000,000	195,800,000
1965	486,200,000	156,000,000	195,360,000
1966	489,600,000	157,000,000	199,760,000
1967	496,400,000	160,000,000	203,280,000
1968	499,800,000	164,000,000	205,480,000
1969	525,300,000	167,000,000	219,560,000
1970	540,600,000	171,000,000	275,440,000

TABLE B.3   (Continued)

1971	576,300,000	182,000,000	311,080,000
1972	576,300,000	186,000,000	337,040,000
1973	661,300,000	216,000,000	375,320,000
1974	1,167,900,000	304,000,000	693,000,000
1975	1,303,900,000	445,000,000	846,120,000
1976	1,392,300,000	580,000,000	854,920,000
1977	1,456,900,000	790,000,000	872,080,000
1978	1,530,000,000	905,000,000	958,320,000
1979	2,148,800,000	1,178,000,000	1,034,000,000
1980	3,670,300,000	1,491,000,000	1,144,000,000

[a]Current dollars per quadrillion BTUs.

[b]Domestic average crude oil wellhead price.

[c]U.S. average wellhead price.

[d]Bituminous coal and lignite price, free on board.

SOURCE: DOE / EIA, *Annual Report to Congress, 1980*, 2:87, 117, and 147.

TABLE B.4 *Losses Due to Regulation by Sector and Fuel*

Year	Change in price ($)	Change in quantity (quadrillion BTUs)	Efficiency loss ($)
Residential / Commercial: Natural Gas			
1973	106,290,000	.37	39,327,300
1974	524,890,000	.27	141,720,300
1975	519,890,000	.15	77,983,500
1976	473,290,000	.43	203,514,700
1977	327,890,000	.71	232,801,900
1978	285,990,000	.79	225,932,100
1979	631,790,000	.10	63,179,000
1980	1,840,290,000	−.05	−92,014,500

TABLE B.4 (Continued)

Industrial: Natural Gas

1973	106,290,000	.08	8,503,200
1974	524,890,000	.25	131,222,500
1975	519,890,000	.77	400,315,300
1976	473,290,000	1.16	549,016,400
1977	327,890,000	1.58	518,066,200
1978	285,990,000	1.82	520,501,800
1979	631,790,000	2.87	1,813,237,300
1980	1,840,290,000	2.63	4,839,962,700

Industrial: Coal

1973	−7,490,000	.29	−2,172,100
1974	181,430,000	.14	25,400,200
1975	164,310,000	−.19	−31,218,900
1976	243,910,000	−.13	−31,708,300
1977	291,350,000	−.05	−14,567,500
1978	278,210,000	−.09	−25,038,900
1979	821,330,000	−.22	−180,330,000
1980	2,232,830,000	−.16	−357,252,800

SOURCE: Calculated from Tables B.2 and B.3, as explained in the text.

Bibliography

Aman, A. C., and Howard, G. S. "Natural Gas and Electric Utility Rate Reform: Taxation Through Rate-Making." *Hastings Law Journal* 28, no. 5 (1977).

American Gas Association. *Demand Market Place Model.* Arlington, Va.: American Gas Association, 1979.

———. *Gas Facts.* Arlington, Va.: American Gas Association, 1978.

———. *Offshore Gas and Oil Supply Model.* Arlington, Va.: American Gas Association, 1977.

———. *Onshore Gas and Oil Supply Model.* Arlington, Va.: American Gas Association, 1978.

Baumol, W. J., and Bradford, D. F. "Optimal Departures from Marginal Cost Pricing." *American Economic Review* 60 (June 1970).

Bethell, Tom. "The Gas Price Fixers." *Harper's* 105 (June 1979).

Bierman, H., Jr., and Hass, J. E. "Inflation, Equity, Efficiency and the Regulatory Pricing of Electricity." *Public Policy* 23, no. 3 (Summer 1975).

Blair, J. P. "The Politics of Government Pricing: Political Influences on the Rate Structure of Publicly-Owned Electric Utilities." *American Journal of Economics and Sociology* 35, no. 1 (January 1976).

Breyer, Stephen, and MacAvoy, Paul W. "The Federal Power Commission and the Coordination Problem in the Electric Power Industry." *Southern California Law Review* 46 (June 1973).

———. "The Natural Gas Shortage and the Regulation of Natural Gas Producers." *Harvard Law Review* 86 (1973): 941.

Bureau of Economic Analysis, U.S. Department of Commerce. *Survey of Current Business*. Washington, D.C.: U.S. Government Printing Office, March 1980 and March 1981.

Bureau of Labor Statistics, U.S. Department of Labor. *Producer Prices and Price Indexes*. Washington, D.C.: U.S. Government Printing Office, 1980, 1981.

Bureau of Mines, U.S. Department of the Interior. *Mineral Industry Surveys*. Washington, D.C.: U.S. Government Printing Office, November 1979.

―――. *Monthly Petroleum Statement*. Washington, D.C.: U.S. Government Printing Office, 1970.

Carron, Andrew S., and MacAvoy, Paul W. *The Decline of Service in the Regulated Industries*. Washington, D.C.: American Enterprise Institute, 1981.

Christensen, L., and Greene, W. H. "Economies of Scale in U.S. Power Generation." *Journal of Political Economy* 84 (1976): 655.

Douglas, George W., and Miller, James C., III. *Economic Regulation of Domestic Air Transport*. Washington, D.C.: Brookings Institution, 1974.

Eckstein, Otto. *The Great Recession, with a Postscript on Stagflation*. Amsterdam: North-Holland; New York: American Elsevier, 1978.

Edison Electric Institute. *Electric Power Survey*. New York: Edison Electric Institute, various years.

―――. "Survey on Construction Work in Progress in Rate Base." New York: Edison Electric Institute, 1978.

Energy Information Administration, U.S. Department of Energy. *An Evaluation of Natural Gas Pricing Proposals*. Washington, D.C.: U.S. Government Printing Office, 1978.

―――. *Annual Report to Congress*. Washington, D.C.: U.S. Government Printing Office, 1980, 1981, vol. 2 and 3.

―――. *Energy Supply and Demand in the Mid-Term: 1985, 1980, and 1995*. Washington, D.C.: U.S. Government Printing Office, 1979.

―――. *Gas Supplies of Interstate Natural Gas Pipeline Companies*. Washington, D.C.: U.S. Government Printing Office, 1978.

Energy Information Administration, U.S. Department of Energy. *Intrastate and Interstate Supply Markets Under the Natural Gas Policy Act*. Washington, D.C.: U.S. Government Printing Office, October 1981.

———. *Monthly Energy Review*. Washington, D.C.: U.S. Government Printing Office, 1974–1982. (Pre-1977 issues published under the Federal Energy Administration.)

English, Michela. "The Problem of Attracting Capital Faced by Investor-Owned Electric Utilities and Possible Regulatory Solutions." New Haven: Yale University School of Organization and Management, Working Paper Series A, No. 38, 1979.

Executive Office of the President. *Economic Report of the President*. Washington, D.C.: U.S. Government Printing Office, 1979–1982.

Federal Energy Administration. *Petroleum Situation Report*. Washington, D.C.: U.S. Government Printing Office, November-December 1978.

Federal Energy Regulatory Commission, U.S. Department of Energy. Form 16 Reports of Gas Supply and Requirements. Washington, D.C.: U.S. Government Printing Office, 1974–1978.

Federal Power Commission. Special Reports. Washington, D.C.: U.S. Government Printing Office, 1972, 1973.

10 Federal Power Service 5–293. "Opinion and Order Prescribing Uniform National Rate for Sales of Natural Gas Dedicated to Interstate Commerce on or After January 1, 1973, for the Period January 1, 1975, to December 31, 1976." Federal Power Commission Opinion Number 770, July 27, 1976.

Freeman, David S. *A Time to Choose*. Cambridge, Mass.: Ballinger, 1974.

General Accounting Office, U.S. Congress. *Problems in the Federal Energy Administration's Compliance and Enforcement Effort*. Washington, D.C.: U.S. Government Printing Office, December 6, 1974.

Gollop, Frank. "The Sources of Growth in the U.S. Electric Power Industry." Paper presented at the Conference on Productivity Measurement in Regulated Industries, 1979.

———, and Jorgenson, Dale. "U.S. Productivity Growth by Industry, 1947–1973." Cambridge, Mass.: Harvard Institute of Economic Research, Paper No. 570, September 1977.

Gordon, Richard. *U.S. Coal and the Electric Power Industry*. Baltimore: Johns Hopkins University Press, for Resources for the Future, 1975.

Hall, Robert, and Mork, Knut A. "Energy Prices and the U.S. Economy 1979–1981." *Energy Journal* 1, no. 1 (April 1980): 41–53.

————. "Energy Prices, Inflation, and Recession, 1974–1975." *Energy Journal* 1, no. 3 (July 1980): 31–63.

Hughes, W. R. "Short-Run Efficiency and the Organization of the Electric Power Industry." *Quarterly Journal of Economics* 76, no. 4 (November 1962).

Joskow, Paul L. "The Determination of the Allowed Rate of Return in a Formal Regulatory Hearing." *Bell Journal of Economics and Management Science* (Autumn 1972): 632–44.

————. "Pricing Decisions of Regulated Firms: A Behavioral Approach." *Bell Journal of Economics and Management Science* 4 (Autumn 1973).

Kalt, Joseph. *The Economics and Politics of Oil Price Regulation.* Cambridge, Mass.: Massachusetts Institute of Technology Press, 1981.

"A Lingering Death." *The New Republic,* June 10, 1978, p. 5.

MacAvoy, Paul W. *Crude Oil Prices: As Determined by OPEC and Market Fundamentals.* Cambridge, Mass.: Ballinger, 1982.

————. *Federal Energy Administration Regulation: Report of the Presidential Task Force.* Washington, D.C.: American Enterprise Institute, 1977.

————. *Price Formation in Natural Gas Fields.* New Haven: Yale University Press, 1962.

————. *The Regulated Industries and the Economy.* New York: W. W. Norton, 1979.

MacAvoy, Paul W., and Noll, Roger. "Relative Prices on Regulated Transactions of the Natural Gas Pipelines." *Bell Journal of Economics and Management Science* 4 (1973): 212.

MacAvoy, Paul W., and Pindyck, Robert S. *The Economics of the Natural Gas Shortage (1960–1980).* Amsterdam: North-Holland; New York: American Elsevier, 1975.

Merrill Lynch, Pierce, Fenner & Smith, Inc., Securities Research Division. "Utility Research: Recent Regulatory Decisions and Trends." 1979.

Nelson, R. A., and Wohar, M. E. "Total Factor Productivity in the Electric Power Industry: A Disaggregated Approach." Newark: University of Delaware, 1980. Mimeographed.

Peltzman, Sam. "Pricing in Public and Private Enterprises: Electric Utilities in the U.S." *Journal of Law and Economics* 14 (April 1971).

Phelps, Charles, and Smith, Rodney. *Petroleum Regulation: The False Dilemma of Decontrol.* Santa Monica, Calif.: Rand Corporation, 1977.

Pifer, H. W., and Scholl, E. L. "An Analysis of Recent Electric Utility Rate Increases." Temple, Baker, and Sloane, Inc., the Energy and Environment Group, June 1975.

Policy and Evaluation, United States Department of Energy. *Reducing U.S. Oil Vulnerability: Energy Policy for the 1980s.* Washington, D.C.: U.S. Government Printing Office, 1980.

"Regulators Propose Breaks for Industry in Low Ceiling for Natural Gas Prices." *Wall Street Journal,* May 10, 1979, p. 3.

Robinson, E. A. G. *The Structure of Competitive Industry.* Chicago: University of Chicago Press, 1958.

United States Congress, House of Representatives. *Report on the Energy Conservation and Oil Policy Act,* 94–340. 94th Cong., 1st sess., 1975.

United States Congress, Senate, Committee on Government Operations. *Hearings on Federal Energy Administration Act.* 93rd Cong., 1st sess., December 1973.

———, Conference Committee. *The Conference Report on Natural Gas,* 95–1126. 95th Cong., 2d sess., 1978.

———, Subcommittee on Synthetic Fuels, Committee on the Budget. Hearings, September 27, 1979.

U.S. Department of Energy. *Statistics of Electric Utilities in the United States.* Washington, D.C.: U.S. Government Printing Office, various years.

Weiss, L. "Antitrust in the Electric Power Industry." In Almarin Phillips, ed., *Promoting Competition in Regulated Markets.* Washington, D.C.: Brookings Institution, 1975.

Wellisz, Stanislaw. "The Public Interest in Gas Industry Rate Structure." *Public Utilities Fortnightly* 70 (July 19, 1962).

Index